The Collected Works of
James M. Buchanan

VOLUME 6
Cost and Choice

James M. Buchanan, 1963

The Collected Works of

James M. Buchanan

VOLUME 6

Cost and Choice

An Inquiry in
Economic Theory

LIBERTY FUND

This book is published by Liberty Fund, Inc., a foundation
established to encourage study of the ideal of a society of free
and responsible individuals.

𒂼𒊏𒄀

The cuneiform inscription that serves as our logo and as the design
motif for our endpapers is the earliest-known written appearance
of the word "freedom" (*amagi*), or "liberty." It is taken from a clay
document written about 2300 B.C. in the Sumerian city-state of Lagash.

01 20 21 23 23 C 6 5 4 3 2
20 21 22 23 24 P 8 7 6 5 4

Library of Congress Cataloging-in-Publication Data
Buchanan, James M.
Cost and choice : an inquiry in economic theory / James M.
Buchanan.
p.   cm. — (The collected works of James M. Buchanan ; v. 6)
Originally published: Chicago : Markham Pub. Co., 1969.
Includes bibliographical references and index.
ISBN 978-0-86597-223-0 (alk. paper). – ISBN 978-0-86597-224-7 (pbk.: alk. paper)
1. Cost.   2. Opportunity costs.   3. Economics—History.
4. Welfare economics.   5. Social choice.   I. Title.   II. Series:
Buchanan, James M.   Works.   1999 ; v. 6.
HB199.B82   1999
338.5′1—dc21   98-32143

LIBERTY FUND, INC.
11301 North Meridian Street
Carmel, Indiana 46032

I, too, sought expression. I know now that my gods grant me no more than allusion or mention.

—Jorge Luis Borges, "Prologue" to *A Personal Anthology*

Contents

Foreword

James M. Buchanan himself speaks of "my little book, *Cost and Choice*." *Cost and Choice* is indeed small in size, but, systematically, it holds quite a central place in Buchanan's work. For the fundamental economic notion of "cost," or "opportunity cost," is intimately related to the individualist and subjectivist perspective that is so essential to the Buchanan enterprise. As a subjectivist, Buchanan insists that opportunity costs exist only in the "eye of the beholder" as envisioned "alternatives" that are never brought into existence. As a methodological individualist, Buchanan believes that opportunity costs cannot be measured in terms of a collective welfare functional aggregating utility foregone across persons.[1]

Similar views in theories of cost have been developed and expressed since the 1930s at the London School of Economics by scholars such as Lionel Robbins, F. A. Hayek, Ronald Coase, and Jack Wiseman. These theories, for systematic as well as personal reasons, have quite strong links to even older theories of the so-called Austrian economists. However, though acknowledging and supporting the Austrian contribution in the socialist calculation debate with arguments based on his own concept of cost, Buchanan distances himself somewhat from the Austrians. Avoiding what he regards as the "arrogance of the eccentric," Buchanan makes a serious effort to integrate his views into the orthodox classical and neoclassical framework. Therefore the discussion in *Cost and Choice* starts with Adam Smith's famous deer-beaver example. In the particularly simple "one-factor" setting of that example, subjective opportunity costs are themselves "explained" by objective transforma-

---

1. James M. Buchanan and G. F. Thirlby, *LSE Essays on Cost* (London: Weidenfeld and Nicholson, 1973), 6; *Cost and Choice: An Inquiry in Economic Theory* (Chicago: Markham Publishing Co., 1969), volume 6 in the series.

tion rates. Because everybody can transform two deer into one beaver and vice versa, any divergence between the transformation and the exchange rate should eventually be washed out by the choices that rational decision makers make in view of the opportunity costs of their decisions. But what about more complicated settings?

Cost and Choice addresses this issue. When publishing the book, Buchanan clearly hoped that other scholars might follow him in his efforts to build a new research tradition in economic analysis around a thorough understanding of the opportunity-cost concept. However, despite Buchanan's serious efforts to communicate his profound insights on the nature of "cost and choice" and to relate these insights to mainstream neoclassical economics, a look at the *Social Science Citation Index* indicates that he did not succeed in this regard. This relative neglect of the theoretical underpinnings of Buchanan's economic worldview as presented in *Cost and Choice* is somewhat strange. After all, specific applications of his general views to problems of public economics were much better received and, in fact, enormously influential.[2] In any event, it might be good policy for those who think highly of Buchanan's more specific insights and arguments to consider more seriously their general foundations as laid out in *Cost and Choice*.[3] The republication of *Cost and Choice* clearly reduces the costs of doing just this and offers ample opportunity to go back to the roots of economics.

Hartmut Kliemt
University of Duisburg
1998

2. In particular, as reprinted in *Debt and Taxes, Externalities and Public Expenditure Theory,* and *Public Principles of Public Debt,* respectively, volumes 14, 15, and 2 of the Collected Works.

3. See also some of the essays in *Economic Analysis,* volume 12 of the Collected Works.

Preface

You face a choice. You must now decide whether to read this Preface, to read something else, to think silent thoughts, or perhaps to write a bit for yourself. The value that you place on the most attractive of these several alternatives is the cost that you must pay if you choose to read this Preface now. This value is and must remain wholly speculative; it represents what you now think the other opportunity might offer. Once you have chosen to read this Preface, any chance of realizing the alternative and, hence, measuring its value, has vanished forever. Only at the moment or instant of choice is cost able to modify behavior.

If you decided a few moments ago that your valuation of the alternative exceeded that expected from reading this Preface, you will have missed this economist's pedestrian prose. But, having rejected it at the outset, you can never know what you will have missed. The benefits that you are now securing from reading the Preface are not comparable with the costs that you would have suffered on choosing the most attractive alternative. These benefits, if there are any, exist. They can be evaluated *ex post*. Costs that are influential for behavior do not exist; they are never realized; they cannot be measured after the fact.

Nonetheless, when you have completed reading this Preface, there is something that will have happened, something that may be valued. You can think about what you might have done with these minutes and, if desired, you can translate these "might have beens" that never were into value terms.

An observer of your behavior, knowing the choice you face, could make an objective estimate of the minutes of resource time that reading this Preface would involve. After your decision he could look at a watch and objectively check out his estimates. If he knew your alternative earnings value, he could place some value on this resource time, a value that would be objective and that would be useful for many purposes of comparison. The observer could not, of course, accurately estimate the value that you might place on your own lost opportunities either before or after choice.

In ordinary discussion, we refer to both your own evaluations and to the observer's as "costs." The external observer of your behavior would say that reading this Preface will or has *cost* you X minutes which he estimates to be worth Y dollars. You would normally say that the same activity "will *cost* X minutes when I might sleep" or "has *cost* X minutes when I might have been sleeping." The point to be noted here is that these several uses of the word "cost" are categorically different. Linguistic usage dictates the same word for several different things. It is little wonder that we find great confusion, especially among economists, about cost.

So much for a summary of this book's main argument. The central notions are simple, and I advance no claim to analytical sophistication. My working hypothesis is that many economists rush headlong into the intricacies of analysis while overlooking certain points of elementary economic logic. Clarification at the conceptual level may be irrelevant for particular applications, and those who are anxious to get on with solving the world's ills may scoff at my insistence on methodological purification. Their skepticism may be increased when they recognize that, in any preliminary confrontation, their own views parallel those developed here. There are few modern economists who would dispute the elementary definition of opportunity cost. Statements that are presumably well understood abound in the standard textbooks.

I suggest that there is likely to be a significant difference between such second-chapter definitions and those which are implied in the analysis that follows. Opportunity cost tends to be defined acceptably, but the logic of the concept is not normally allowed to enter into and inform the subsequent analytical applications. My aim is to utilize the theory of opportunity cost to demonstrate basic methodological distinctions that are often overlooked and to show that a consistent usage of this theory clarifies important areas of disagreement on policy issues. In public finance alone, debates over tax incidence, tax capitalization, public-debt burden, and the role of cost-benefit analysis can be partially resolved when protagonists accept common concepts of cost. The unsatisfactory state of welfare economics can at least be understood and appreciated more adequately when the incorporated cost confusions are exposed. The once heated and long smouldering debate over the possibility of socialist calculation emerges with perhaps a different glow. Something can be said about such currently relevant topics as the draft and crime. None of these or any other possible policy applications will be discussed in exhaustive detail. Some such discussions would require a book at least as long as this to untangle the knots that cost-theory ambiguities have tied.

My secondary purpose is to trace the evolution of ideas in the conception of cost. Largely because of its relative neglect by modern economists, I emphasize the contributions that stem from a London School of Economics tradition, a tradition that has not been generally recognized and one which even its own members have taken more or less for granted.

Latter-day Austrians especially may suggest, with some justification, that the theory developed is properly labeled "Austrian." Beyond question, an important source of the London conception is Austrian. But as I read the early Austrians along with the London contributions, I remain convinced that uniquely characteristic features were added and that the whole construction reached operational viability only in London. By way of illustrating this point, much of what seems to me to be orthodox cost theory can be traced directly to its Austrian sources. According to my readings and interpretation, Wicksteed deserves credit for providing a source of the distinctly nonorthodox LSE tradition that is equally or perhaps more important than the Austrian. American followers of H. J. Davenport, whose own ideas on cost were highly perceptive, did not generate a tradition comparable to London's.

The basic sources of the modern London tradition are represented in papers by Robbins, Hayek, and Coase in the 1930's. These are followed up insistently by the much neglected writings of Thirlby which extend from 1946 through 1960. Additional papers in the tradition were published by Jack Wiseman in the 1950's. These published materials seem, however, to be only the now-visible residues of an extensive dialogue that must have been part-and-parcel of economic teaching at LSE over a span of some thirty years.

The first chapter sketches out the doctrinal history of cost theory before the 1930's. Chapter 2 discusses the origins and development of the London theory, and Chapter 3 summarizes the theory of opportunity cost in two contrasting analytical settings. The remaining chapters in the book are devoted to applications. Chapter 4 examines cost theory in public finance, the application that aroused my own interest in the need for conceptual clarification. Chapter 5 uses opportunity-cost logic as a means of looking again at the Pigovian welfare norms. Chapter 6, the most important as well as the most difficult of the book, demonstrates the relevance of basic cost theory in the whole domain of nonmarket decision-making.

Acknowledgments

I consider myself fortunate to be able to regard Frank H. Knight as "my professor," and his influence on my thinking is more direct in this book than in my other works. Both his insistence on getting fundamental ideas straight and his important contributions to cost theory have provided inspirations for my efforts.

More specifically, I should here acknowledge the help of many students, colleagues, and fellow scholars. Students in 1965 and 1967 graduate seminars at the University of Virginia suffered with me during the critical periods when my confusions were at their peaks. In 1967 an early draft was circulated, and I was fortunate in securing much useful revision advice. In this respect, I appreciate the help provided by William Breit, R. H. Coase, F. A. Hayek, Mark Pauly, Roger Sherman, G. F. Thirlby, Gordon Tullock, Richard E. Wagner, Thomas Willett, and Jack Wiseman. Although they probably did not realize it, both Francesco Forte and S. H. Frankel provided encouragement in discussions at critical times when my own enthusiasm wavered.

As on numerous other occasions, my work on this book was facilitated at many stages by my secretary Betty Tillman, whose loyalty and devotion are rarely matched in this increasingly impersonal world of academic scholarship.

J. M. B.
Los Angeles
March 1969

Cost and Choice

1. Cost in Economic Theory

Classical Economics

> If among a nation of hunters . . . it usually costs twice the labour
> to kill a beaver which it costs to kill a deer, one beaver should nat-
> urally exchange for or be worth two deer.[1]

The classical theory of exchange value is summarized in this statement. Adam Smith was not so careful as his modern counterpart who states his assumptions precisely, but perhaps this is why we still enjoy reading *The Wealth of Nations*. Normal or natural value in exchange is determined by the relative costs of production. This answers the central questions of classical economics.

Costs are calculated in units of resource input. "It usually costs" means that a specific resource outlay is required, an outlay that can be estimated in advance with some accuracy and measured *ex post* either by the resource owner or by an external observer who doubles as cost accountant. The relative costs of producing are objectively quantifiable, and no valuation process is necessary. Given a standard for measurement, relative costs can be computed like the relative weights of apples or potatoes. In Smith's elementary and conjectural model, the standard for measurement is a unit of homogeneous labor time. There are no nonlabor inputs (no other "negative goods"). The production functions for both deer and beaver are linear and homogeneous; that is to say, deer and beaver are available in unlimited supply at prevailing relative cost ratios.

---

1. Adam Smith, *The Wealth of Nations* (New York: Random House, Modern Library Edition, 1937), p. 47.

Even in so simple a model, why should relative costs determine normal exchange values? They do so because hunters are assumed to be rational utility-maximizing individuals *and* because the positively valued "goods" and the negatively valued "bads" in their utility functions can be identified. If, for any reason, exchange values should settle in some ratio different from that of cost values, behavior will be modified. If the individual hunter knows that he is able, on an outlay of one day's labor, to kill two deer or one beaver, he will not choose to kill deer if the price of a beaver is three deer, even should he be a demander or final purchaser of deer alone. He can "produce" deer more cheaply through exchange under these circumstances. By devoting one day's time to killing a beaver and then exchanging this for deer, he ends up with three deer, not two. Since all hunters can be expected to behave in the same way, no deer will be produced until and unless the expected exchange value returns to equality with the cost ratio. Any divergence between *expected* exchange value and *expected* cost value in this model would reflect irrational behavior on the part of the hunters.

In this interpretation, the classical theory embodies the notion of opportunity cost. To the hunter at the point of an allocative decision, the cost of a beaver is two deer and the cost of a deer is one-half a beaver. At an expected exchange ratio of one for two, each prospective hunter must be on the margin of indifference. Physical production and production-through-exchange yield identical results. Labor time, the standard for measurement, is the common denominator in which the opportunity costs are computed.

Realized exchange value need not be equal to *realized* cost value in the elementary deer-beaver model or in the classical model generally. As interpreted here, there must be competitive indeterminacy in the allocation of resources to deer and beaver production. If, relative to prevailing demand patterns, a large number of hunters choose to produce beaver on a particular day, the price or market value of beaver will fall below cost. Or, alternatively, if the demand pattern shifts suddenly while the allocation of resources remains substantially unaltered, the same result can be forthcoming. Price, which is *realized* exchange value, can and will diverge from realized cost value. When this happens, however, some of the hunters will look back at the time of decision and conclude that mistakes were made.

There is one-way causality in this deer-beaver model. Relative costs determine normal exchange values. Implicitly, the theory assumes that predictions about production relations, the ratios of inputs to outputs, are considerably more accurate than predictions about demand patterns. This converts the theory into an elegant operational hypothesis. *Objective*, external measurements can be introduced which should yield predictions about normal exchange values. These predictions can be falsified.

The theory contains no prediction of normal exchange value when production is not possible, that is, when supply is fixed. Here normal exchange value, like realized exchange value in all cases, is set by the forces of demand. But to Adam Smith, this would not have embodied a predictive theory. No behavioral tendency can be introduced that relates the values of "goods" one to the other in terms of some objectively identifiable common denominator. For such fixed-supply goods, Smith would have said, simply, that no theory of value exists. Viewed in this context, J. S. Mill's infamous statement that nothing more could be said on the theory of value can be interpreted somewhat more sympathetically than modern economists have been wont to do.

Exchange value tends to equality with objectively measurable cost of production. This is a positive proposition and carries with it no normative content. Nothing is said or implied to the effect that market price *should* equal cost of production. In the direct sense, classical economics does not contain a normative theory of allocation. The equalization of return to similar units of resources tends to emerge from the basic postulate of rational behavior along with the implicit identification of "goods" and "bads" in the utility functions of individuals.

The interpretation sketched out above is unfair to those who have criticized classical economics. Confusions abound on many points of analysis. Once the extreme simplifications of Smith's homogeneous and single input model are dropped, the problems commence. The intricacies of classical reasoning are centered around the search for a comparable common denominator of value when inputs (negative goods) are heterogeneous. Ricardo's genius was not up to this challenge despite valiant efforts. Rent theory explained away, though somewhat unsatisfactorily, the return to land. But differing labor-capital ratios remained, and Marx's resort to "socially necessary" labor time was a retreat into the circularity that the whole classical theory was designed to circumvent.

Smith and, finally, Ricardo were both forced to rehabilitate the theory's pragmatic relevance at the expense of its elegance. Heterogeneous units of input were measured in the money prices established in factor markets. The cost of production for a good was computed in money. As an elementary explanation of the normal or natural exchange value for a specific good, the essential features of the deer-beaver model continue to hold. The normal exchange value of a pair of shoes tends to equal $10 if $10 is the money cost of producing shoes, the necessary outlay made to owners of all resource inputs. Unfortunately, the elegance and the objectivity of the deer-beaver world have disappeared in this more realistic cost-of-production model. The objective opportunity cost of a beaver in Smith's model is two deer because it "usually" takes twice as much physical input to produce a beaver. In the more realistic setting, what is the opportunity cost of a pair of shoes? Costs are measured in a numeraire and these reflect *values* of physical inputs. The direct connection between these inputs and alternative outputs is gone. To say that payments to resource owners amount to $10 does not, at least directly, imply that alternative products valued at $10 could be produced.

If costs are $10, the producer must expect a value of at least $10. The postulate of rational behavior along with the presumption that the numeraire is positively desired still implies that expected value be equal to or above costs. But what now determines costs? No longer is the theory simple enough to concentrate our attention on one moment of decision, one act of choice. Instead of this, we now must think of a chain of interlinked decisions over varying quantities of output, over separate time periods, and over many decision-makers. The producer, facing a near-certain outlay of $10, must expect a value in excess of this figure if he is to choose to produce. But resource owners, who are now conceptually separated from the producer-entrepreneur, must also make choices. Why does the unit mix of inputs sum to $10? Exchange values are established for resource units in markets, and each owner must be assumed to expect values in excess of costs when he makes a unit of resource available. But what are his costs? The classical economists were forced to discuss the costs of producing primary resources.

They thought themselves successful to an extent with respect to labor of an unskilled or common variety. In Smith's elementary model, the cost of a beaver is two deer, which for comparative purposes is measured as a day's labor, the time required to kill either of the alternatives open to the hunter. The cost of common labor time is the corn that is required to nourish the laborer and to allow him to reproduce his kind. Again, this corn can be measured in labor time required to produce the corn. But the analytical differ-ence between these two statements is great, and in the latter we see a false extension of a basically correct theory of exchange value. The opportunity-cost theorem that is central to the deer-beaver model almost wholly disap-pears in the theory of wages for common labor. A day's labor time measures the cost of a beaver because it represents the genuine alternative product, two deer. A half-day's labor time presumably measures the cost of a laborer, not because it represents any genuine alternative product, but because it repre-sents the *outlay* that is required to nourish him. The input-output relation has been subtly changed from that found in the simpler model. The labor input that measures the cost of a beaver is that required to produce an *alter-native,* two deer. And no hunter would kill beaver unless the appropriate ra-tio of expected value holds. The outlay that may actually be required to kill a beaver is irrelevant to realized exchange value. By contrast, in the classical theory of wages, no consideration of the alternative to producing a laborer is included. Even the most sympathetic critic will find it difficult to read opportunity-cost thinking into the analysis.

It was perhaps in recognition of the difficulty here that both Smith and Ricardo shied away from rigorous analysis in discussing wages. A classical theory of sorts emerged which related wages to levels of subsistence. In this theory of wages based on Malthusian population principles, the cost theory of exchange value has lost almost all of its opportunity-cost moorings. Wages of common labor tend to subsistence levels, not because this is a predictable result of rational individual behavior, but because of the natural checks of famine and pestilence. The relationship between exchange value and individ-ual choice behavior has been severed—and with it the essential logic of any cost-of-production theory. This classical theory of wages is almost devoid of behavioral content.

A source of some confusion that runs through and sometimes dominates classical discussion of cost has not been mentioned. This is the notion of *pain cost,* often called *real cost.* Not content with searching for a predictive theory of exchange value, the classical writers sought to "explain" the emer-gence of value in some basic philosophical sense. The toil and trouble, the physical pain, involved in working seemed to "justify" the payment of wages. Observation revealed that capital also received payment. Hence, the concept of abstinence developed by Senior seemed to place the capitalist alongside the wage-earner as a recipient of justifiable rewards. The importance of this real-cost doctrine in sowing confusion should not now be underestimated. Even today the theory of comparative advantage as taught by many sophisticated analysts contains its manifest nonsense, although fortunately little damage is done.[2]

Cost does reflect pain or sacrifice; this is the elemental meaning of the word. But we must recognize the linguistic problem which confronts economists in the use of the word "cost" to refer to quite separate things. Any opportunity within the range of possibility that must be foregone in order to select a preferred but mutually excluding alternative reflects "costs" when it is "sacrificed." And its rejection must involve *pain* despite the fact that differentially greater pleasure is promised by the enjoyment of the mutually exclusive alternative. Cost and pain are far from being opposites, contrary to what loose discussion often seems to suggest; the concept of cost as pain or sacrifice is and must be central to the idea of opportunity cost. In certain aspects of the classical treatment, this pain-as-sacrifice concept was understood. As mentioned, the cost of capital accumulation was discussed in terms of "abstinence": by abstaining from consuming, capital is allowed to accumulate. Clearly, this involves opportunity-cost reasoning.

For the most part, however, the real-cost or pain-cost notion in classical economics refers to something quite different. *Pain* also arises when nothing is sacrificed in a behavioral context. Pain occurs when, as a result of a past chain of events, the utility of the individual is reduced without offsetting pleasures. The required outlay of labor may involve pain, something that can within limits be measured by sweat, muscle fatigue, and tears. The transfer of capital assets to meet a debt obligation, to pay taxes, or to pay tribute to a highwayman also involves pain, again something that can be proximately measured by a decrement in net worth on the individual's balance sheet. In this second sense, pain cost has no connection with deliberately sacrificed alternatives. The expectation of such pain may inform the comparison of alternative opportunities for choice, but the realization of such pain is irrelevant either in explaining or in justifying value. This vital distinction between

2. Even in 1967 economists need to be warned of the fallacy. On this, see Royall Brandis, "The Myth of Absolute Advantage," *American Economic Review*, LVII (March 1967), 169–74.

the two separate notions of pain cost was not recognized by the classical economists or by many of their successors. The roots of many modern ambiguities lie in the classical failure to note this distinction, a failure that neo-classical economics did not remove satisfactorily.

Marginal-Utility Economics

A revolution in value theory took place after 1870. The classical cost-of-production theory was replaced by the marginal-utility theory, as the latter was variously developed by William Stanley Jevons, Karl Menger, and Leon Walras. These theorists were somewhat less obligated than their classical predecessors to define costs precisely for the simple reason that costs assumed much less importance for them in explaining exchange value. At least in the elementary stages of analysis, they seemed willing to accept classical definitions: Their quarrel with the classicists was not centered on the notion of cost. They considered their differences to be more profound. Regardless of the manner in which costs were defined, however, the marginal-utility theorists rejected classical analysis.

The development of a *general* theory of exchange value became a primary concern. Classical analysis was rejected because it contained two separate models, one for reproducible goods, another for goods in fixed supply. The solution was to claim generality for the single model of exchange value that the classical writers had reserved for the second category. Exchange value is, in all cases, said the marginal-utility theorists, determined by marginal utility, by demand. At the point of market exchange, all supplies are fixed. Hence, relative values or prices are set exclusively by relative marginal utilities.

If the revolution had amounted to nothing more than this, it would have scarcely warranted notice. The contribution of these theorists was not the mere substitution of a utility for a cost theory of exchange value. In the process of effecting this substitution, they were forced to develop the idea that values are set *at the margin*. In this manner, they were able to resolve the diamond-water paradox; value-in-use and value-in-exchange were no longer possibly contradictory. The economic calculus was born.

Nonetheless, there were losses in discarding the classical apparatus. In their search for a general theory, the marginal-utility economists largely abandoned a predictive theory of normal exchange value. They provided a satisfactory explanation of realized value; they did little toward developing analysis of expected or natural value. In the strict sense, theirs is a logical theory, not a scientific hypothesis capable of refutation. And as with all general theories, the marginal-utility theory explained too much.

The generality carried some secondary benefits, however, and a logical extension was the marginal-productivity theory of distribution. Since goods are valued in accordance with relative marginal utilities, resources should also be valued in accordance with the values of their final-product components. There was no call to go beyond the fixed supply of resources in a first approximation. For almost a century, the theory of population was dropped from the economist's kit of tools.

Marginal-utility economics is often called "subjective-value" economics, and the doctrinal revolution also carries this name. The classical cost-of-production theory was *objective* in the sense that external measurements of comparative costs were thought to provide predictions about normal exchange values of commodities. The replacement of this with a theory that explained relative exchange values by relative marginal utilities necessarily implies a loss of objective empirical content. Marginal utilities, however, were acknowledged to be dependent on quantities, and, for the whole group of demanders, on the supplies put on the market. Hence, even with a full knowledge of demand conditions, normal exchange values could not be predicted until and unless predictions were made about relative supplies. The cost or supply side of value had to be brought in. A one-sided explanation was no longer possible; demand-supply economics became a necessity.

Given a supply of a commodity, exchange value was determined by marginal utility, as worked out in a market interaction process. But utility is a subjective phenomenon, and it is not something that can be externally or objectively measured, as can classical cost-of-production. To understand this, let us think of a world of two commodities, each of which is in fixed supply, say, the world of bear and raccoon. Both are "goods," and each good is available in predictably fixed quantity in each period. If we know with accuracy the demand or marginal-utility schedules for all demanders, exchange value can be predicted. Note, however, that this prediction does not emerge as an outcome or result of a rational behavior postulate, at least in the same sense as the classical deer-beaver model. Suppose, given the fixed supplies along with the demand patterns, it is predicted that one bear will exchange for two raccoons. If realized values are observed to be different from those predicted, it is the result only of inaccuracy in the initial data upon which the predictions were made. No equilibrating mechanism is set in motion; there is no sense of error as there is in the deer-beaver model. No corrective process will emerge; values as realized are always "correct"; errors arise only in the data used by the observer. The marginal-utility theory in its elementary methodology here is akin to the simple Keynesian model of income determination. By contrast and despite its flaws, the classical cost-of-production theory is more closely analogous to the Swedish theory of income determination where expectations can explicitly enter the analysis.

To introduce elements of a predictive theory of exchange value required a return to quasi-classical analysis. Costs of production were acknowledged to influence exchange value through their effects on supply. And in discussing costs, the marginal-utility theorists could accept a money measure without ambiguity since they had no reason to search for a common denominator of physical resource inputs. The necessity of paying for inputs arises because these represent components of value in final products. This approach leads almost directly to opportunity-cost reasoning.

The value or price of resource units represents, especially for the Austrians (Menger, Böhm-Bawerk, Wieser), the value of product that might be produced by the same resource units in alternative uses or employments. This is the price that the user or employer of resources must advance in order to attract the resources away from such alternative opportunities. At the level of decision for the resource owner, the implicit opportunity-cost notion is identical to that which is present in Smith's deer-beaver model. To the Austrians, and notably to Wieser, rational behavior on the part of resource owners ensured the equalization of return in all employments.

Jevons was unique among the subjective-value theorists in his treatment of cost, and he is considerably more classical than Austrian. The cost of producing involves "pain," a concept that was almost entirely absent from Austrian discussion. This pain cost can be discussed in terms of marginal disutility. Jevons was thus the complete marginalist, and, for him, all choice reduced to a comparison of utilities and disutilities at the margin. He was able to resolve the diamond-water paradox through the use of, essentially, the classical apparatus. Because he did not sufficiently generalize the alternate-product conception, his cost theory was inferior to that of the Austrians or even to that which was implicit in Smith. Nonetheless, Jevons did concentrate attention on the act of economic choice, and this might have influenced Wicksteed in his major advances toward his wholly modern conception.

To the early Austrian theorists, costs of production are measured in money, and these reflect the value of output that *might have been produced* if the same resource inputs had been rationally applied in alternative employments. This is indeed an opportunity-cost notion, but it is subjective only in the sense that values of goods are set by their relative marginal utilities to demanders. Since these values are set in organized markets, they can be objectively measured.

The Marshallian Synthesis

Alfred Marshall thought that he had rewritten classical economics, incorporating, in the process, qualifications and criticisms which apparently were developed independently of the marginal-utility theorists, despite the similarities in treatment of particular elements. His period analysis provided a general model in which adjustment lags determined the relative explanatory power of marginal-utility and cost-of-production hypotheses. His sympathies were with the classicists, and he sensed the predictive advantages of the basic classical model.

Marshall was too sophisticated an analyst to overlook the simple idea of opportunity cost, but explicit statements of this notion cannot readily be found in his discussion. Cursory reading suggests that Marshall was willing to accept a naive classical version of real or pain cost arising from the exertions of the laborer and the abstinence of the capitalist. In part, his lack of precision in defining cost was due to his direct and pragmatic concern with explaining price formation. Marshall did not ask conceptual and definitional questions for their own sake, and he seemed willing to stop short of these inquiries once he had provided what he considered satisfactory answers to relevant practical questions.

For these purposes, money costs, as determined by prices set in factor markets, were sufficient. In the long period, after all adjustments are made and if other things do not change in the interim, prices tend to settle at the level of money costs when constant returns prevail. To Marshall this was a reasonably satisfactory statement, really all that could be expected from economics. His models, here as elsewhere, are often "fuzzy"—one feels deliberately so—not because he overlooked, but because he recognized the complexities involved in setting things all straight. Perhaps this is unduly sympathetic to Marshall, but one feels that, despite the ambiguities, he would never have made the blunders that his successors fell into over their failures to define costs properly.

Frank Knight and American Neoclassical Paradigms

In sharp contrast to Marshall stands Frank Knight whose "main concern is the correct definition of the problem. . . ." He sensed the ambiguities that were present in the neoclassical, essentially Marshallian, treatment of cost. In a series of important papers written in the late 1920's and early 1930's, he established the conception of opportunity or alternate-product cost that became the paradigm for modern price theory, notably in its American-Chicago variant. Starting with Adam Smith's deer-beaver model, Knight demonstrated its inherent opportunity-cost content along the lines that I have sketched at the beginning of this chapter. "[T]he cost of beaver is deer and the cost of deer is beaver, and that is the only objective and scientific content in the cost notion."[3] The opportunity cost of a *commodity* is measured in units of alternate or *displaced product* and "all references either to 'sacrifice' or 'outlays' [should be] simply omitted."[4] "[C]ost must be measured in terms of products, and not of pains or outlays."[5]

In this 1928 statement of what he considered to be the "correct" definition, Knight was following what he later acknowledged to be the standard Austrian position, especially that represented in Wieser. He also indicated in a later paper that this position was shared by Wicksteed. The cost of producing a unit of a commodity is simply measured by the alternative real product that *might have been* produced had the resource inputs used in production been rationally reallocated to other uses. The market value of these alternate products provides a common denominator for estimation, a value that is de-

3. Frank H. Knight, "A Suggestion for Simplifying the Statement of the General Theory of Price," *Journal of Political Economy*, XXXVI (June 1928), 359.
4. Ibid., 355.
5. Ibid., 363.

termined in the exchange process. Knight seems to have been correct in claiming this approach akin to that of Wieser who said: "Since each productive process diminishes this possession, it reduces utility—it *costs,* and it costs exactly as much as the value which the material and labor required would have produced if rationally applied."[6]

Within a few years, however, Knight sensed that something was wrong with his straightforward alternate-product measure of opportunity cost. In papers published in 1934 and 1935, he tried to spell out his misgivings, but without great success.[7] He tried to modify the alternate-product definition of cost to take account of the differences in the irksomeness of different resource uses, especially with application to the allocation of labor. In an extremely complex argument, Knight claimed that to the extent that resource owners do not equalize pecuniary returns to resource units in all uses, the principle of alternate-product cost does not wholly apply. If the deer hunter accepts a relatively lower pecuniary reward for his more pleasant work, a dollar's worth of resource payment withdrawn from deer production and transferred to beaver production will increase "social" product by more than one dollar. Hence, the opportunity cost of the resultant increase in beaver production is more than the market value of the deer that the resource inputs might have produced before the transfer. Thus, the net change in irksomeness must also be acknowledged and counted.

This is surely a reasonable and fundamentally correct observation. It reflects, nonetheless, a notion of opportunity cost quite different from that which Knight had earlier advanced. The introduction of nonpecuniary advantages and disadvantages of resource uses severs the critically important link between the objectively measured market value of alternate product and the cost that enters into the subjective calculus of the decision-maker. This

6. F. von Wieser, "The Theory of Value," *Annals of The American Academy of Political and Social Science,* II (March 1892), 618. See also F. von Wieser, *Über den Ursprung und die Hauptgesetze des wirtschaftlichen Werthes* (Wien, 1884), p. 100.

7. Frank H. Knight, "The Common Sense of Political Economy (Wicksteed Reprinted)," *Journal of Political Economy,* XLII (October 1934), 660–73, reprinted in Frank H. Knight, *On the History and Method of Economics* (Chicago: University of Chicago Press, Phoenix Books, 1963), pp. 104–18. This is a review article of the two-volume edition of Wicksteed. Frank H. Knight, "Notes on Utility and Cost" (Mimeographed, University of Chicago, 1935). Published as two articles in German in *Zeitschrift für Nationalökonomie* (Vienna), Band VI, Heft 1, 3 (1935).

linkage is essential if the theory of value is to retain scientific content in any predictive sense. Without realizing it, Knight necessarily shifted from a positive model of behavior in which costs are objectively measurable into a logical model of choice in which costs are purely subjective. In the latter model, which has no predictive content, the *market value* of the displaced or alternate product has no direct relevance for the resource owner's decision. Hence, this value cannot in any way be considered as the measure of *his* cost. Properly interpreted, as Wicksteed came close to saying, the *predicted* or *expected* value of the alternate product at the moment of decision and as estimated by the chooser is the cost. And, under this definition, the *nonmarket* value of the alternate conditions of employment is included as an essential part of cost.

The initial position taken by Knight became the orthodox one, and it remains so in the major part of modern price theory. The opportunity-cost notion is central. "The cost of any alternative (simple or complex) chosen is the alternative that has to be given up; where there is no alternative to a given experience, no choice, there is no economic problem, and cost has no meaning."[8] "Economic cost, then, consists in the renunciation of some 'other' use of some resource or resource capacity in order to secure the benefit of the use to which it is actually devoted."[9] "The only general-cost theory which can be maintained will, after all, be that of alternative cost, best formulated as displaced product cost, but this must be stated subject to the qualification that it is true only 'in so far' as at equilibrium the indicated conditions obtain."[10]

In the context of most theoretical discussion, these are perfectly acceptable and wholly correct statements. Cost is measured by the market value of displaced product. Cost is objective in that it can be estimated, at least in *ex post* terms, by external observers, despite the fact that market values are set, generally, by the subjective evaluations by many producers and consumers. Market prices measure collective evaluations at the margins of production, and prices are themselves objective.

8. Knight, "Notes on Utility and Cost," op. cit., p. 18.
9. Ibid., p. 19.
10. Knight, "The Common Sense of Political Economy (Wicksteed Reprinted)," op. cit., p. 116.

These statements about cost are widely and uncritically accepted by most modern price theorists, most of whom fail to see that opportunity cost, so defined, has no connection with choice at all. It is precisely for this reason that the simple but subtle differences between this orthodoxy and the alternative London theory provide suitable subject matter for a small book.

2. The Origins and Development of a London Tradition

Wicksteed and the Calculus of Choice

Wicksteed deserves recognition for having shifted cost theory away from its classical, objective foundations. Although Jevons can with justice be labeled as precursory, the major advance beyond Marshallian conceptions was made by Wicksteed, who tied opportunity cost quite directly to choice. He stated that cost-of-production, "in the sense of the historical and irrevocable fact that resources have been devoted to this or that special purpose, has no influence on the value of the thing produced."[1] In this respect, cost-of-production does not affect supply. What does affect supply is anticipated cost "in the sense of alternatives still open which must now be relinquished in order to produce this specific article";[2] this cost "influences the craftsman in determining whether he will produce it or not."[3] Here, the critical relationship between any measurement of cost and the act of choice is established. At any moment in time, one can look either forward or backward. One looks backward in time in a perspective of foreclosed alternatives. One looks forward in time in a perspective of alternatives that still remain open; choices can be and must be made. With this elementary clarification, cost tends to be a part of choice among alternatives, a choice that must be subjective to the chooser. Cost does not hold the direct relationship to commodity or resource units that it does in both the classical and neoclassical discussion.

1. Philip H. Wicksteed, *The Common Sense of Political Economy* (London: Macmillan, 1910), p. 380.
2. Ibid.
3. Ibid.

Wicksteed fully recognized the many ambiguities that surrounded the usage of the term "cost," and he provided excellent examples.[4] But when all is said, Wicksteed, too, remained less than wholly clear. When put to it, he chose to define cost-of-production or cost-price as "the estimated value, measured in gold, of all the alternatives that *have been sacrificed* in order to place a unit of the commodity in question upon the market"[5] (italics supplied).

There is no doubt that Wicksteed was a major formative influence on the cost theory that emerged in the late 1920's and early 1930's at the London School of Economics. And, as I hope to show, traces of the "correct" theory of cost are found in the acute observations of Wicksteed. This may not emerge full-blown in Wicksteed for the simple reason that he need elaborate no further in answering his own questions. One feels that Wicksteed's cost theory, as that of Marshall, could have been made fully equal to the challenge presented by the new range of issues of the 1930's.

H. J. Davenport

Herbert J. Davenport was an American economist and, roughly, a contemporary of Wicksteed. His influence was limited to a relatively small group of followers, none of whom were major figures in the history of doctrine. Davenport's insights on opportunity cost, however, if read from the perspective developed in this book, suggest that it is appropriate to place his name between that of Wicksteed and Knight in this summary review.

Davenport's emphasis was on what he called "entrepreneur's cost," and he clearly defined this in a utility dimension. "That is to say, cost as a margin determinant is purely a matter within the personal aspects of entrepreneurship, a managerial fact, a subjective phenomenon, in which all the influences bearing on the psychology of choice between different occupations and leisure have their place."[6] Furthermore, Davenport explicitly recognized that

4. "These reflections will explain the great ambiguity of the term 'cost price.' . . . [M]embers of the same trade . . . will use the word in different senses. One will declare that he is 'making no profits at all,' but is 'selling at a loss,' and another will say that 'things are bad enough with him, but not quite so bad as that,' when they both mean to indicate exactly the same state of affairs. Men will declare in good faith that they are 'selling below cost price,' and yet will never think of suspending operations." Ibid., pp. 380–81.

5. Ibid., p. 385.

6. Herbert J. Davenport, *Value and Distribution* (Chicago: University of Chicago Press, 1908), p. 273.

cost is related to the particulars of the choice situation, and, indeed, his emphasis on entrepreneur's cost stemmed from his criticism of other writers, notably Marshall, who confused this with what Davenport called "collectivist cost."[7]

Embedded in Davenport's treatise, *Value and Distribution,* is a conception of opportunity cost that is almost as sophisticated as that developed by Wicksteed. The failure of Davenport's ideas to have more influence than they did have was due, apparently, to his failure to articulate these ideas and also perhaps to his petulance toward the idols of the profession in his time. Davenport would have surely come into his own had he been able to criticize the more flagrant confusions in cost theory that emerged only after the 1920's.[8]

Knight on Cost as Valuation

It is interesting that before he had written any of the papers previously cited, Frank Knight had explicitly referred to cost estimation as a valuation process inherent in choice itself. "[T]he cost of any value is simply the value that is given up when it is chosen; it is just the *reaction or resistance to choice* that makes it choice"[9] (italics supplied). Having made this tie-in between opportunity cost and the decision process, however, Knight tended to confuse the fundamental issues in his later emphasis on alternate-product value, a value determined, presumably, not by the chooser, but in the whole market process.

Robbins, 1934

In a basic paper published in 1934,[10] Lionel Robbins reacted against the emphasis by Knight and others on an alternate-product conception of oppor-

---

7. See esp. ibid., p. 404.

8. For a summary of the history of cost theory in which Davenport's ideas are prominently featured, see Bob M. Keeney, "The Evolution of Cost Doctrine" (Mimeographed, Midwestern Economics Association, November 1967).

9. Frank H. Knight, "Fallacies in the Interpretation of Social Cost," *Quarterly Journal of Economics,* XXXVIII (August 1924), 592f., reprinted in F. H. Knight, *The Ethics of Competition* (London: Allen and Unwin, 1935), p. 225.

10. L. Robbins, "Certain Aspects of the Theory of Cost," *Economic Journal,* XLIV (March 1934), 1–18. Robbins' interest in the issues here was indicated in his earlier paper, "On a

tunity cost, much as Knight himself was led to do in his 1934 and 1935 papers. In so doing, Robbins provided the basis for an opportunity-cost conception that later came to be identified with the London School of Economics. Neither Knight in his 1924 paper nor Robbins realized the importance of the distinction they were making, and Robbins considered himself to be merely clarifying certain ambiguities that had arisen in connection with the emerging Austrian orthodoxy, the source of which he attributed to Wieser. Specifically, Robbins argued that cost must be defined in terms of displaced *value* and not in terms of displaced *real product*. He demonstrated that once beyond the Smithian deer-beaver model, displaced real product has little meaning. His illustrative examples were those of final goods produced with wholly different inputs or with the same inputs but in differing and fixed coefficients. Shifts in demand generate shifts in cost under such conditions, and these cannot be interpreted in terms of displaced real-product alternatives. Costs are changed because the relative *values* of the inputs change, values derived from the demand for final products.

Although these clarifications were useful and represented the main thrust of Robbins' argument, they are not the subject of interest here. More or less as asides, Robbins introduced several statements that involve a different basic notion of cost. He apparently did not think of these statements in this light, perhaps because they were especially obvious to one who had fully learned his Wicksteed and perhaps because, in another sense, they were immaterial to his central theme. I refer to his explicit linking of cost to the act of choice itself. "The process of valuation is essentially a process of choice, and *costs are the negative aspects of this process*" (p. 2, italics supplied). "[I]t is the central requirement of any theory of cost that it should explain the *actual* resistances which production in any line of industry encounters" (p. 5, italics in original). "The isolated producer thinks of the *sacrifice* that he is making by not producing something else" (p. 5, italics supplied).

Unfortunately, after having interspersed these highly provocative remarks in his discussion, Robbins proceeded, almost simultaneously, to obscure their potential impact. In this, Robbins seems to have proceeded much as Knight had a decade before. On the page immediately following the last two state-

Certain Ambiguity in the Conception of Stationary Equilibrium," *Economic Journal*, XL (June 1930), esp. 209–11.

ments cited above Robbins said: "The condition that prices shall be equal to cost of production in the value sense is as essential a condition of equilibrium in the Walrasian system as the condition that marginal products shall be proportionate to factor prices" (p. 6). The subtle but essential distinction between cost in the act of choice and cost in the predictive theory of economic behavior has disappeared in this apparently orthodox neoclassical statement.

Mises, Robbins, and Hayek on Calculation in a Socialist Economy

As I suggested in the Preface, latter-day Austrians can with some legitimacy claim that the concept of opportunity cost, here attributed to Jevons, Wicksteed, Davenport, Knight, and ultimately developing into a London tradition, was independently developed by later Austrians and notably by Ludwig von Mises. In his monumental, polemic, and much neglected treatise, *Human Action*,[11] Mises advances a theory of opportunity cost that is, indeed, almost equivalent to the full-blown LSE conception to be described later. Mises' explicit treatment of cost in *Human Action* will also be discussed later. At this point it is noted only that the German treatise that provides the basis for the English-language work was not published until 1940. For the period in question, therefore, Mises' earlier writings must be examined. In this connection, specific reference must be made to his 1920 paper, in which he argued that economic calculation in a socialist society is impossible,[12] and to his book which followed in 1922.[13]

A modern reading of these early contributions by Mises suggests that some of the intuitive force of his argument stemmed from a more sophisticated conception of opportunity cost than he was able to make explicit at that time. Mises' attack on the possibility of socialist calculation is wholly consis-

11. Ludwig von Mises, *Human Action* (New Haven: Yale University Press, 1949).

12. "Die Wirtschaftsrechnung im sozialistischen Gemeinwesen," *Archiv für Sozialwissenschaften*, XLVII (1920), reprinted as "Economic Calculation in the Socialist Commonwealth," in F. A. Hayek (ed.), *Collectivist Economic Planning* (London: Routledge, 1935).

13. Ludwig von Mises, *Die Gemeinwirtschaft* (Jena, Germany: Gustav Fischer, 1922). The second German edition appeared in 1932. Mises added an epilogue to this edition at the time of its translation as *Socialism* (New Haven: Yale University Press, 1951).

tent with the conception of opportunity cost that emerged more fully later, both at LSE and in his own writings. Although he did not center his early argument directly on the cost problem, *per se,* the general tenor of Mises' discussion is clearly and quite closely related to later developments in cost theory, and his contribution to that theory surely deserves recognition alongside those of Wicksteed and Knight. Quite apart from the importance of Mises' own works is his influence on the work of Lionel Robbins and F. A. Hayek, the transplanted Austrian who became one of the central figures of the LSE tradition.

In addition to writing the 1934 paper previously cited, Robbins also participated in the great debate over the possibility of socialist calculation.[14] An assessment of his contribution at this stage must be closely connected with the assessment made of Mises' work. Robbins' argument might well have been based on a more sophisticated notion of opportunity cost than that which is explicitly discussed, but one senses in a modern reading that, along with Mises and Hayek, he could have been much more effective if he had been able to make more articulate the distinction between objectively measurable cost and cost as an element of a decision process.

Hayek's specific contribution to the development of cost theory that is contained in his part of the debate on socialist calculation is a peculiarly mixed bag. In his "Introduction" to the famous collection of essays,[15] Hayek foreshadows his later and more explicit methodological emphasis on the necessity of distinguishing between the subjective apparent sense data of the person who chooses in the economic process and the objective data that are available to any external observer. As we shall see, this methodological step is essential to any genuine understanding of cost. It appears, however, that Hayek had not in 1935 incorporated this methodology fully into his own basic theory. In his essay, "The Present State of the Debate," included in the collection, he suggests clearly that cost of production becomes difficult to calculate in a socialist setting primarily because of the absence of the conditions of competitive equilibrium where "cost of production had indeed a

14. Lionel Robbins, *The Great Depression* (New York: Macmillan, 1934), esp. pp. 143–54.

15. F. A. Hayek (ed.), *Collectivist Economic Planning,* op. cit.

very precise meaning."[16] This emphasis, which was also evident in Robbins' work, left the way open for Lerner's effective reply which argued simply for the adoption of a rule for setting prices at marginal opportunity costs, regardless of the state of the world.[17]

My purpose here is not to evaluate the discussion of socialist calculation, but only to examine that discussion for the contributions it contains to the pure theory of opportunity cost. With the exception of Lerner (whose insight was much more profound, and who was himself a part of the developing LSE tradition), those who argued that socialist calculation is possible accepted an objective definition of cost without any serious critical examination of the issues that such definition might raise.

Hayek, Mises, and Subjectivist Economics

F. A. Hayek was appointed Tooke Professor of Economic Science and Statistics at the London School of Economics in 1931 and held this chair until 1950. Along with Robbins, he must be credited with providing the source of much of the LSE tradition in cost theory, a tradition that seems to have emerged gradually over these two decades. As suggested above, Hayek's contribution was primarily that of providing the underlying methodological basis for the more explicit works on cost by others. He presented the methodology of subjectivist economics with convincing authority; his essays remain recommended reading almost thirty years after their initial publication. And economic theory, generally, should certainly have avoided some major modern confusions if Hayek's essays had been more widely read and understood.

A distinction must be made between the orthodox neoclassical economics which incorporates the *subjective-value* or marginal-utility revolution in value theory and the *subjectivist economics* of the latter-day Austrians, notably Mises and Hayek. The dependence of price (value) on marginal utility, subjectively determined, can be fully recognized, while essentially an *objective* theory of cost is retained. In Jevons' famous statement, marginal utility depends on

16. Ibid., p. 226.
17. A. P. Lerner, "Statistics and Dynamics in Socialist Economics," *Economic Journal,* XLVII (June 1937), 253–70.

supply which, in its turn, depends on cost of production. As stated, this theory is wholly objectivist in character, although, of course, the valuation of buyers and sellers is incorporated as a part of the objective data. Costs are objectively determinable, although the theory does not say that costs alone determine value. As contrasted with classical theory, one-way causality is missing, but not the objectivity of the explanation. It is this latter objectivity that is jettisoned, wholly and completely, by both Mises and Hayek. In this respect, they differ sharply with earlier Austrians, although they do not seem fully to sense the distinction. In many respects, they seem much closer to Wicksteed than to Wieser.

There seems no doubt that subjectivist economics was explicitly introduced at LSE by Hayek. In a paper of major importance, published in 1937,[18] he laid down the central features of the subjectivist methodology, features that he elaborated in considerably more detail in later works.[19] In his 1937 paper, Hayek gives credit to Mises for the latter's background work,[20] published in German in 1933, but made available only much later (1960) to English-language scholars. Hayek's initial paper provides, in one sense, the "classical" methodology of the subjectivists, a methodology which is central to a theory of cost that is related directly to choice and that is to be contrasted with the theory of cost embodied in neoclassical orthodoxy.

The subtle distinction between the economics of subjective value and the subjectivist economics espoused by Hayek and Mises was quite naturally obscured so long as the task of economic theory was largely limited to the explanation of market interactions. The famous Jevons statement about supply serves as an illustration. So long as individual producers, responding to the demands of consumers, are the actors whose behavior we seek to explain, there is really no need of inquiring as to whether the costs of production are subjective or objective. Costs are obstacles to the choices of producers, and

18. F. A. Hayek, "Economics and Knowledge," *Economica*, IV (1937), 33–54, reprinted in Hayek, *Individualism and Economic Order* (Chicago: University of Chicago Press, 1948), pp. 33–56.

19. Additional essays that appeared in 1940, 1941, 1942, and 1943 are included in the two volumes, *Individualism and Economic Order*, op. cit., and *The Counter-Revolution of Science* (Glencoe, Ill.: The Free Press, 1952).

20. Ludwig von Mises, *Grundprobleme der Nationalökonomie* (Jena, Germany: Gustav Fischer, 1933), translated by George Reisman as *Epistemological Problems of Economics* (New York: Van Nostrand, 1960).

economists can discuss "laws of cost" in this context without presuming that objective measurement is possible.

With the advent of "welfare economics," regardless of how this might be defined, such previously admissible methodological fuzziness no longer passes muster. If idealized market interaction process—pure or perfect competition—is used as the standard for deriving conditions which are then to be employed as norms for interference with actual market process, the question of objective measurement must be squarely faced. If prices "should" be brought into equality with costs of production, as a policy norm, costs must be presumed *objective*, in the sense that they can be measured by others than the direct decision-maker.

Only Hayek and Mises seemed to be completely aware of this problem and of its major importance, although many other economists seem to have been vaguely disturbed by it. *Subjectivist economics*, for Hayek and Mises, amounts to an explicit denial of the *objectivity* of the data that informs economic choice. The acting subject, the chooser, selects certain preferred alternatives according to his own criteria, and in the absence of external change he attains economic equilibrium. This personalized or Crusoe equilibrium is, however, wholly different from that which describes the interactions among many actors, many choosers. In the latter case, the actions of all others become necessary data for the choices of the single decision-maker. Equilibrium is described not in terms of objectively determined "conditions" or relationships among specific magnitudes, e.g., prices and costs, but in terms of the realization of mutually reinforcing and consistent expectations. The difference between these two approaches, the objectivist and the subjectivist, is profound, but it continues to be slurred over in the neoclassical concentration on the idealized market interaction process in which all individuals behave economically. In an unchanging economic environment populated by purely economic men, the two approaches become identical in a superficial sense. In a universe where all behavior is not purely economic, where genuine choice takes place, the important differences emerge with clarity.

At this juncture in the development of economic theory, we must, I think, ask why the convincing arguments of Hayek exerted so little weight. Without question, objectivist economics continues to carry the day, and few of its practitioners pause to examine critically its methodological foundations. There are, no doubt, several reasons for this failure, but undue attention paid to the definition of equilibrium, although of immense importance in itself, may have retarded acceptance of the more general subjectivist notions. Neutral readers of the impassioned debates on socialist calculation might have been led to think that the central issue was really one that involved the possibly erroneous derivation of policy criteria from stationary equilibrium settings. Indeed this is an issue, but the subjectivist critique is obscured here. As noted earlier, this concentration on equilibrium, of which Hayek, Robbins, and to a lesser extent Mises, all are guilty, left the way open for Lerner to drop all references to general equilibrium in his derivation of the policy rules that explicitly require the introduction of objectively measurable costs.

The Practical Relevance of Opportunity Cost: Coase, 1938

Alongside the more abstract and methodological contributions to cost theory made by Robbins, Hayek, and Mises, other elements of perhaps a more authentic LSE tradition emerged in the 1930's. These reflect the direct application of some of the basic Wicksteed notions to problems that confront the businessman. This "common sense" approach had its roots at LSE in the work of Cannan who continually insisted on starting with problems as they exist. Cannan does not seem to have made specific contributions to cost theory, although he accepted opportunity-cost notions readily.[21]

This practical-business approach was further promoted by Arnold Plant who seems to have contributed significantly, but indirectly, to the development of the London tradition. Plant did not, to my knowledge, treat cost theory explicitly in any of his published works, but the contributions made by his students and colleagues reflect his influence. Both R. H. Coase and G. F. Thirlby, whose contributions are summarized below, were Plant's students.

The contrast between the accountant's definition-measure of cost and that of the neoclassical economist is standard fare. But this contrast—when the full meaning of opportunity cost is incorporated—takes on features that are even now outside the orthodox economist's kit of tools. This can be seen

---

21. See esp. his review of Henderson's *Supply and Demand*, reprinted in Edwin Cannan, *An Economist's Protest* (London: P. S. King, 1927), pp. 311–14.

clearly in a series of articles by R. H. Coase, published in 1938, which were written specifically for the enlightenment of accounting practitioners.[22] These papers remain known to relatively few modern economists despite their exceptionally clear discussion of definitional problems involved in using the term "cost" and their necessary and emphatic insistence that cost be related to the choice process.

"The first point that needs to be made and strongly emphasized is that attention must be concentrated on the variations which will result if a particular decision is taken, and the variations that are relevant to business decisions are those in costs and/or receipts" (p. 106). "It should be noted that accounting records merely disclose figures relating to past operations. Business decisions depend on estimates of the future" (p. 108). "[C]osts and receipts cannot be expressed unambiguously in money terms since courses of action may have advantages and disadvantages which are not monetary in character, because of the existence of uncertainty and because of differences in the point of time at which payments are made and receipts obtained" (p. 116). "The cost of doing anything consists of the receipts which could have been obtained if that particular decision had not been taken. When someone says that a particular course of action is 'not worth the cost,' this merely means that he prefers some other course—the receipts of the individual, whether monetary or nonmonetary does not matter, will be greater if he does not do it. This particular concept of costs would seem to be the only one which is of use in the solution of business problems, since it concentrates attention on the alternative courses of action which are open to the businessman. Costs will only be covered if he chooses, out of the various courses of action which seem open to him, that one which maximizes his profits. *To cover costs and to maximize profits are essentially two ways of expressing the same phenomenon*" (p. 123) (italics supplied).

A careful, modern reading of these early papers by Coase indicates that

22. R. H. Coase, "Business Organization and the Accountant," *The Accountant* (October–December 1938). These articles are reprinted in David Solomons (ed.), *Studies in Costing* (London: Sweet and Maxwell, 1952), pp. 105–58.

Along with Coase, other members of Plant's group of young business economists were R. S. Edwards, R. F. Fowler, and David Solomons. This group was interested in making economic theory of greater practical relevance for business operations and especially for accounting practice.

the concept of cost embodied in them is conceptually distinct from the neo-classical paradigm. Coase quite explicitly ties cost to choice, and he rejects any attempt to classify costs into categories—e.g., fixed and variable—independently of the identification of the decision under consideration. Perhaps the most significant contribution, for our purposes, is contained in the italicized statement cited above. Any profit opportunity that is within the realm of possibility but which is rejected becomes a cost of undertaking the preferred course of action. Despite the necessity of accepting this straight-forward result of apparently consistent opportunity-cost reasoning, econo-mists were—and are—extremely reluctant to take this step. To include all foregone profits as costs plays havoc with the whole cost-curve apparatus that is a part of our stock-in-trade. And without this how could we teach elementary price theory?

In the strict neoclassical model, costs are distinguished sharply from fore-gone profits because they are not tied *directly* to choice. Costs are objectively measurable outlays, approximated by the value of alternate product. It is use-ful to keep the classical foundations of the analysis in mind here. Costs, to the extent that they are objective and, hence, externally measurable by an outsider who stands apart from the choice process, provide the basis for a predictive hypothesis about the behavior of acting individuals (firms) and, through this, a hypothesis about prices. The neoclassical objectivist world and the London-Austrian subjectivist world cannot readily be reconciled.

Confusion was confounded by the Robinson-Chamberlin and related con-tributions in the early 1930's just when the more basic notions in cost theory seemed on the way to being clarified. These contributions elevated the the-ory of the firm to a position of undue importance in a model that apparently embodied the objectivist rather than the subjectivist notions of cost. If the purpose of analysis is to "explain" the behavior of the firm, choice must be the subject of attention, and costs cannot be objectified. The whole marginal-revenue–marginal-cost apparatus, strictly speaking, remains a part of a cen-tral *logic of choice* and nothing more because, to the effective decision-taker, both costs and benefits are evaluated in purely subjective terms. It is little wonder that modern developments in the theory of the firm have been con-cerned with relaxing the artificial and apparent objectivity of cost and reve-nue streams by substituting more plausible, even if largely nonoperational, utility indicators.

Coase's early work on the theory of the firm was within a choice-explanatory context and without the constraints of the more widely acclaimed contributions of the imperfect and monopolistic competition models. In this context, Coase was fully correct in his argument that foregone profits must be included in opportunity cost and in his insistence that cost be considered as that which can be avoided by not taking a particular decision.

Despite his major contribution toward clarifying the concept of opportunity cost in the context of the theory of the firm, Coase did not in his 1938 papers fully incorporate the "subjectivist economics" of Hayek and Mises into his analysis, nor did he draw the distinction between his concept and that embodied in neoclassical orthodoxy.[23]

G. F. Thirlby and "The Ruler"

Academically, both Vienna and Capetown were close neighbors to London in the 1930's, and, as a consequence of the influence of transplanted LSE economists, the next major contribution to the theory of cost emerged in Capetown. Primarily under the influence of Arnold Plant and W. H. Hutt, an oral tradition developed at Capetown which expanded the London approach. The published results appeared in 1946 in two papers by G. F. Thirlby. In these papers, Thirlby, who had been trained at LSE and who returned to London a few years later, carried forward the process of clarification. He continued until 1960 his attempts to convert other economists to what he considered to be a more acceptable and consistent view of opportunity cost, but his argument seems to have been largely neglected.

In his first 1946 paper, Thirlby, like Coase, related the economist's notions

23. In his later, and more widely known, paper on marginal-cost pricing, Coase's argument for the multi-part tariff was informed throughout by the conception of opportunity cost developed in his earlier papers. His emphasis, as it has been interpreted by later writers, was, however, on the familiar conflict between marginal-cost and profitability criteria. His opportunity-cost defense of multi-part pricing has been largely overlooked. See R. H. Coase, "The Marginal Cost Controversy," *Economica*, XIII (August 1946), 169–82. In a comment on Coase's paper, G. F. Thirlby criticized the implied objectivity of cost. See G. F. Thirlby, "The Marginal Cost Controversy: A Note on Mr. Coase's Model," *Economica*, XIV (February 1947), 48–53.

on cost to those of the accountant.[24] Thirlby had fully incorporated the sub-jectivist economics of Wicksteed and the latter-day Austrians in his analysis, and his emphasis was on the subjectivity of costs. Citation at some length from this early paper seems warranted here:

> To the subjectivist, cost would be understood to refer to the prospective opportunity displaced by the administrative decision to take one course of action rather than another. Cost is inevitably related to the behavior of a person. The person is faced with the possibility of taking one or other of (at least) two courses of action, but not both. He considers the relative significance to him of the two courses of action, and finds that one course is of higher significance than the other. He 'prefers' one course to the other. His prospective opportunity of taking the less-preferred course becomes the prospective cost of his taking the more preferred course. By deciding to take the preferred course, he incurs cost—he displaces the alternative opportunity. The cost is not the things—*e.g., money—which will flow along certain channels* as a result of the decision; it is the loss, prospective or realized, to the person making the decision, of the opportunity of using those things in the alternative courses of action. *A fortiori*, this cost *cannot be discovered by another person who eventually watches and records the flow of those things along those channels.* Cost is not something which is objectively discoverable in this manner; it is something which existed in the mind of the decision-maker before the flow began, and something which may quite likely have been but vaguely apprehended. . . .
>
> Cost is ephemeral. The cost involved in a particular decision loses its significance with the making of a decision because the decision displaces the alternative course of action (italics in original).[25]

Thirlby's emphasis on the ephemeral nature of cost distinguishes his paper from earlier contributions in the LSE tradition. And in this early paper, Thirlby himself wavers in his adherence to this conception which his later writings were to stress. Note that he says "prospective or realized" at one

24. G. F. Thirlby, "The Subjective Theory of Value and Accounting Cost," *Economica*, XIII (February 1946), 32–49.
25. Ibid., 33–34.

point: he fails to see that the very notion of realized cost produces a contradiction, as he was later to demonstrate. Similarly, his reference to cost being "vaguely apprehended" implies that something different from that which is apprehended emerges at a later point in the decision-action sequence that might be called cost.

The extension of Thirlby's rigorous opportunity-cost reasoning to the question of the relevance and practicability of the so-called "rules" for pricing was straightforward, and this was the content of his second paper, "The Ruler."[26] Thirlby made it clear that he was relatively uninterested in the much debated "which rule" question, one that obscures the analysis of the "any rule" problem. As in his other paper, stress was placed on the fact that cost was not "an objective something in the sense that it can be scrutinized." The standard definitions and measurements were held to omit valuations of the "lost opportunities," and Thirlby argued that unless these were taken into account, no rule could ever be applied to ensure the satisfactory meeting of people's preferences.

He rejected the orthodox distinction between "long run" and "short run," and he was explicit in saying that "cost occurs only when decisions are made, that is, in planning stages" (p. 259). He clarified the distinction between what we might call the decision, budget, and accounting levels of calculation. Cost is relevant to decision, and it must reflect the value of foregone alternatives. A budget, however, reflects the prospective or anticipated revenue and outlay sides of a decision that *has been made*. It is erroneous to consider such prospective outlays as appear in a budget as costs. The budget must, however, also be distinguished from the account, which measures realized revenues and outlays that result from a particular course of action. This clarification is a simple one in itself, but it is highly useful for our purposes. It shows that the forward-looking or *ex ante* framework is not, in itself, sufficient to ensure the adoption of the appropriate cost concept. The budget is, by definition, a planning document, an *ex ante* projection of events; it does not, however, balance anticipated revenues against anticipated *cost* in the relevant opportunity-cost sense. The "cost" side of a budget measures

26. G. F. Thirlby, "The Ruler," *South African Journal of Economics,* XIV (December 1946), 253–76.

anticipated *outlays* which are to be made as a result of a particular course of action's having *already* been chosen. It cannot reflect the value of alternative courses of action which might have been selected save in the exceptional case where no alternative revenues in excess of anticipated outlay could be secured.

There is, or should be, no difficulty in convincing critics that cost must be subjective at the moment of choice. But one can fully accept the subjectivist point of view in this respect and still think that, after decision, cost *becomes* objective and, hence, measurable. In his earlier paper, Thirlby might not have fully sensed the instantaneous vanishing of cost upon decision. In "The Ruler," however, this point is emphasized. "[T]he cost figure will never become objective; i.e., it will never be possible to check whether the forecast of the alternative revenue was correct, because the alternative undertaking will never come into existence to produce the actual alternative revenue" (p. 264).

Following these two 1946 papers, Thirlby continued to present his ideas on cost, for the most part in the context of a theory for business organization and decision. Although most of the central ideas were developed in the two early papers, some shifts of emphasis are worth noting. In a 1952 paper, Thirlby argued plausibly for a more widespread recognition of a time dimension in economic analysis, particularly with respect to the decision process. "[A] period of time elapses between the making of the decision and the achievement of the results. . . . A mental deliberation or planning operation, followed by a decision, precedes the business operations which are so planned." Recognition of this would "keep in front of our minds the high degree of subjectivity in the maximization process. . . . It would prevent our attributing a false objectivity to the cost and revenue figures."[27]

In his latest paper, published in 1960, Thirlby suggests that subtle shifts in the definition of cost lead to confusion about social cost. "The subtle change in the meaning of cost, from the valuation of his *own* [the entrepreneur's] displaced end-product to the money input required for the selected course of action, is a change leading to still another conception, which carries with it the suspicion that it is to be regarded as a social cost. It resembles the first

---

27. G. F. Thirlby, "The Economist's Description of Business Behavior," *Economica*, XIX (May 1952), 150.

meaning of cost, in that it is supposed to be an alternative value displaced, but differs from it in that it is not the entrepreneur's *own* valuation of his *own* displaced end-product, but other people's (consumers') valuations of products which might have been produced by other entrepreneurs had they not been displaced."[28] This statement accurately summarizes the distinction between the London conception of opportunity cost and the orthodox conception that is currently held by most economists.

Mises' *Human Action*

As I noted earlier, Ludwig von Mises was one of the chief sources for the subjectivist economics expounded at LSE by Hayek, and his work was an influence as well on both Robbins and Thirlby. Mises' earlier work on the possibility of socialist calculation has been mentioned; some reference must now be made to his treatise, *Human Action*,[29] published in English in 1949, but based on a work in German published in 1940. In this book, Mises does discuss cost explicitly, even if briefly, and his basic conception is similar to that London conception that is best represented in Thirlby's work. Generically, "costs are equal to the value attached to the satisfaction which one must forego in order to attain the end aimed at" (p. 97). "At the bottom of many efforts to determine nonmarket prices is the confused and contradictory notion of real costs. If costs were a real thing, i.e., a quantity independent of personal value judgments and objectively discernible and measureable, it would be possible for a disinterested arbiter to determine their height. . . . Costs are a phenomenon of valuation. Costs are the value attached to the most valuable want-satisfaction which remains unsatisfied" (p. 393).

Mises' ideas on cost have been further developed by two of his American followers. In his two-volume treatise, *Man, Economy, and the State,* Murray Rothbard adopts a subjectivist conception of cost that is closely akin to that advanced by G. F. Thirlby.[30] And perhaps the single most satisfactory incor-

---

28. G. F. Thirlby, "Economists' Cost Rules and Equilibrium Theory," *Economica,* XXVII (May 1960), 150.

29. Mises, op. cit.

30. See Murray Rothbard, *Man, Economy, and the State* (New York: Van Nostrand, 1962), esp. Vol. I, pp. 290–308.

poration of a choice-related notion of cost into a general price-theory context is found in Kirzner's *Market Theory and the Price System*.[31]

The Death of a Tradition?

At the London School of Economics, the ideas on cost developed by Robbins, Hayek, Coase, Thirlby, and others formed a part of a developing oral tradition which included many participants. Modern adherents to this tradition seem scarce, however, and only Jack Wiseman fully qualifies. In two basic papers published in the 1950's, Wiseman tried as others had earlier tried to apply LSE opportunity-cost logic to the long-discussed problems of marginal-cost pricing, applying this logic both as general criteria for organizing a collectivist economy and as the specific criterion for public-utility enterprise.[32]

Wiseman shifted from LSE to York in 1963 and Thirlby retired from active academic life in 1962. There remain, no doubt, residues of the opportunity-cost tradition at LSE, but this does not inform the mainstream in either the teaching of economic theory or in the scholarly contributions of staff members. In the United States, the influence of Mises and his latter-day Austrian followers seems peripheral to the modern mainstream of economic theory. The concept of opportunity cost which emerged from both the subjectivist-Austrian and the common-sense approaches—the concept that blossomed for two decades at LSE—seems to have lost in its struggle for a place among the paradigms of modern economics. Along with other conundrums in intellectual history, this is not easy to explain. The arguments have not been refuted, and within their limits they surely remain valid. Hopefully, this book will generate a partial resurrection by delineating the methodological foundations of the two parallel theories of economic process.[33]

---

31. See I. M. Kirzner, *Market Theory and the Price System* (New York: Van Nostrand, 1963), esp. Chapter 9.

32. Jack Wiseman, "Uncertainty, Costs and Collectivist Economic Planning," *Economica*, XX (May 1953), 118–28; and his "The Theory of Public Utility Price—An Empty Box," *Oxford Economic Papers*, IX (February 1957), 56–74.

33. The manuscript for this book was completed before I had access to the article on "Cost" by A. A. Alchian in *International Encyclopedia of the Social Sciences*, III (New York: Macmillan, 1969), pp. 404–15.

Appendix to Chapter 2: Shackle on Decision

A survey of London contributions would be incomplete without reference to the work of G. L. S. Shackle. The problem of integrating intellectual constructions within one's own thought is well illustrated in his case. Shackle was a student at LSE in the years when the opportunity-cost conception was being developed. In several of his papers, Thirlby expresses indebtedness to Shackle; and it is immediately evident that Shackle's treatment of the decision process is wholly consistent with the London doctrine of opportunity cost. Yet—and surprisingly—Shackle does not, to my knowledge, make the obvious linkage between his provocative and important work on decision, uncertainty, and time and the work on opportunity cost carried forward by his LSE counterparts. In his general treatment of cost itself, Shackle reverts to orthodoxy.

His contributions to the theory of decision can, nonetheless, be helpful in clarifying the theory of cost, and some selected excerpts from one of his books[34] seem worth presenting:

> When a number of actions, distinguished from each other by the sets of outcomes respectively assigned to them, are *available* and choice amongst them is open to the decision-maker, the sets of outcomes, each considered as a whole, are mutually exclusive rivals of each other. Within each set, the members also are mutually exclusive rival hypotheses. Thus these outcomes cannot be matters of fact but are things imagined by the decision-maker. They exist in his imagination, not after but *before* his commitment to a particular act; their existence is within the moment of decision and forms part of that act [pp. ix, x].

> *Decision* means literally a cut . . . a cut between past and future [p. 3]. . . . We assume that choice amongst a set of rival available acts will be made in view of consequences associated in some manner and degree by the decision-maker with the acts. We also assume that the only consequences relevant for this choice are experiences of the decision-maker. . . . For three separate reasons . . . they cannot be experiences coming from outside the

34. G. L. S. Shackle, *Decision, Order and Time in Human Affairs* (Cambridge: Cambridge University Press, 1961), pp. ix, x.

decision-maker's mind from sources of stimulus observable in principle by others; they cannot, that is to say, be what we ordinarily speak of as 'real' experiences requiring the intervention of sense perceptions of the external world; they cannot be 'news' [p. 8].

. . . Outcomes are figments and imaginations [p. 9]. For it is the contention that the outcomes, by comparison of which decision is made, are figments of the individual mind (no matter whether in some later actuality they shall be observed to have come true: nothing could be more irrelevant) [p. 10].

These and many other statements by Shackle could be inserted almost without change in the cost discussions of Coase and Thirlby. Shackle's failure to make the shift of these relevant ideas to his own—though much more elementary—discussion of cost indicates that the classically based predictive theory can exist alongside the logical theory of choice in the thought patterns of a single economist, even though the two theories are incompatible with each other.

3. Cost and Choice

A century has elapsed since the subjective-value revolution in economic theory, but the subjective theory of value has not been fully reconciled with the classically derived objective theory. As the notes on the development of the concept of opportunity cost indicate, economists have not drawn carefully the distinction between a predictive or scientific theory and a logical theory of economic interaction. As subsequent chapters will demonstrate, this methodological confusion is the source of pervasive error in applied economics. The treatment and discussion of cost, especially in its relation to choice, provides a usefully specific context within which the more general methodological issues can be examined.

The Predictive Science of Economics

From its classical origins, economics has laid claim to classification as a predictive science. This means that conceptually refutable hypotheses are embodied and that the refutations of these hypotheses can command ultimate recognition by competent professional scientists. To qualify under this restriction, the science must have objective, empirical content. Something must be measurable—at least conceptually—which will allow either the corroboration or the refutation of the central propositions. The basic elements of economic theory are, of course, the actions of human beings. The science consists in the efforts to predict the effects on human behavior induced by specific changes in environment. Operationality dictates that the behavioral responses be objectively measurable.

Consider the elementary proposition that relative prices rise when relative costs increase, subject to the standard *ceteris paribus* qualifications. This proposition is derived from the postulate that individuals behave "economically," that they seek to minimize "costs" and to maximize "benefits" or "revenues." But this postulate remains empirically empty until specific descriptive content is given to "costs" and to "benefits" or to "revenues." The behavioral postulate is that of *economic* man. If this is dropped, the predictions are drained of power.

It is important that the limitations as well as the strengths of this predictive theory be noted. There is no implied presumption that men *should* behave economically. Properly interpreted, the theory's claim is limited to making predictions on the "as if" assumption that men do so behave in some average or representative sense. The motivational assumption is vital in that this allows the scientist to use the objectively observable magnitudes of money cost and money revenue streams as representations of the subjectively evaluated alternatives of choice in individuals' behavior patterns. As experience has shown, considerable success has been achieved in this genuinely scientific theory of economic behavior. Men do behave economically in sufficient degree to allow many predictions to be corroborated. But the oversight of the basic limitations of the predictive theory has led to major error in normative application.

The orthodox neoclassical model of market process is one in which the acting units behave economically. To the extent that the model approximates reality, the objectively observed cost and revenue streams accurately represent the dimensionally different and subjectively evaluated alternatives among which choices are actually made by individuals. To this same extent, and only to this extent, specific relationships among costs, as objectively observed, and prices, as objectively observed, can be predicted to describe the equilibrium toward which the whole process converges. Note especially that these relationships, these conditions of equilibrium, are themselves derivative predictions based on the motivational postulates of the model. For example, equalities between prices and marginal costs, as objectively observed quantities in fully competitive equilibrium, are inferred predictions which depend on the behavioral assumptions upon which the whole theory is constructed. These equalities have no normative significance, and they have no direct relationship to allocational efficiency. The methodological muddle in modern economics is perhaps most clearly revealed by the unwarranted crossing of the bridge between the inferential predictions of the genuinely scientific theory and the normative conclusions about efficiency that are so often drawn.

This may be illustrated in a variation, similar to that used by Knight in his papers previously cited, upon the simplest of models, Adam Smith's deer and beaver model. The objective conditions of the model remain as before. One day's labor is required to kill a deer and two days' labor to kill a beaver. Objectively measurable costs are in a one-for-two ratio. The prediction is made that exchange values will settle in a two-for-one ratio, a ratio which will be described by the equalities between marginal costs and prices. Let us suppose, however, that the relative price ratio exhibits no tendency to move toward the equilibrium level that is predicted; prices do not tend toward equality with marginal costs. Only the most naive of welfare economists should conclude from this that the allocation of resources is inefficient. Instead he probably would introduce, as Knight did, the possibility that hunters, generally, may have some nonpecuniary or noneconomic arguments in their utility functions. Marginal costs, as these affect choice behavior, may then not be the same as the simply observed ratios of labor time. The welfare economist, presuming only that the market is competitively organized, then concludes that the price-marginal cost equalities are satisfied in the equilibrium that he observes, despite the variations from objectively based predictions.

In resorting to noneconomic arguments in the utility function to rectify his falsified predictions, however, the economist has shifted the whole analysis from a predictive to a nonpredictive and purely logical theory. Objectively observable cost-revenue streams cannot serve as surrogates for the subjectively evaluated alternatives in which noneconomic elements are influential. The inferred predictions of relationships that characterize equilibrium positions are falsified. No potential gains-from-trade are indicated if these predictions are not fulfilled. No welfare improvements could, therefore, be expected from rearrangements designed to ensure that the predicted relationships will be produced.

The implications of all this for modern welfare economics could scarcely be underestimated. My argument suggests that almost all of this subdiscipline has been based on simple methodological confusion. It has converted predictive propositions into allocative norms which have then been used to make policy proposals. Some of the more specific instances of this confusion will be discussed in subsequent chapters.

In one sense it might be said that the neoclassical economist has succumbed to the temptation to make his whole theory more general than its methodology warrants. This temptation has been increased by the parallel, and equally confused, logical theory of economic choice, which itself is completely general but which lacks predictive content. This purely logical theory, sharply distinct from the classical in its predictive implications, finds its origins in the subjective-value theorists, but its more explicit sources are Wicksteed, the later Austrians, and the economists associated with the London School of Economics. In full flower, this is the "subjectivist" economics espoused by Hayek and Mises to which I earlier made reference. Some reconciliation between the genuinely scientific theory of economic *behavior* and the pure logic of *choice* is required. The achievement of this reconciliation is one of the major purposes of this exploratory study in which the notion of opportunity cost becomes the analytical coupling device.

Cost in the Predictive Theory

If we remain strictly within the predictive science of economics, cost can be considered to be properly defined in most of the modern textbooks, and there is little need to elaborate on these standard definitions. This is the cost of the familiar textbook diagrams, the objectively identifiable magnitude that is minimized. It is the market value of the alternate product that might be produced by rational reallocation of resource inputs to uses other than that observed. This market value is reflected in the market prices for resource units; hence, cost is measured directly by prospective money outlays.

For whom is this cost relevant? This becomes a critically important question. Cost as just defined is faced in the strict sense only by the automaton, the pure economic man, who inhabits the scientist's model. It is the behavior-inhibiting element that is plugged into the purely mechanistic market model. The conversion of objective data reflecting prospective money outlays into the subjective evaluations made by real-world decision-makers is of no concern to the predictive theorist. In the strict sense, this theory is not a theory of *choice* at all. Individuals do not choose; they behave predictably in response to objectively measurable changes in their environment.

Cost in a Theory of Choice

The distinction between the concept of cost in the predictive context, as sketched out above, and the concept of cost in a more general theory of choice, as articulated—though not fully—in Chapter 2, can best be emphasized at this point by elaborating this second concept. The essential element in this concept is the direct relationship between cost and the act of choice, a relationship that does not exist in the neoclassical predictive theory. In the London-Austrian conception, by contrast, cost becomes the negative side of any decision, the obstacle that must be got over before one alternative is selected. Cost is that which the decision-taker sacrifices or gives up when he makes a choice. It consists in his own evaluation of the enjoyment or utility that he anticipates having to forego as a result of selection among alternative courses of action.

The following specific implications emerge from this choice-bound conception of cost:

1. Most importantly, cost must be borne exclusively by the decision-maker; it is not possible for cost to be shifted to or imposed on others.
2. Cost is subjective; it exists in the mind of the decision-maker and nowhere else.
3. Cost is based on anticipations; it is necessarily a forward-looking or *ex ante* concept.
4. Cost can never be realized because of the fact of choice itself: that which is given up cannot be enjoyed.
5. Cost cannot be measured by someone other than the decision-maker because there is no way that subjective experience can be directly observed.
6. Finally, cost can be dated at the moment of decision or choice.

In a theory of choice, cost must be reckoned in a *utility dimension*. In the orthodox predictive theory, however, cost is reckoned in a *commodity dimension*. This distinction can be applied to each of the six attributes listed above. In a theory of choice, cost represents the anticipated utility loss upon sacrifice of a rejected alternative. Because utility functions are necessarily personal, cost is tied directly to the chooser and cannot exist independently of him. In the predictive theory of economic behavior, the cost of producing one "good" is the amount of another that could be produced instead. Cost, as such, exists independently of the choice process, and there is no direct linkage between choosing and bearing cost.

Cost, then, is purely subjective in any theory of choice, whereas cost is objective in any theory that involves genuine prediction. If cost is to influence choice, it must be based on anticipations; it cannot be based on realized experience—at least directly. On the other hand, once cost is divorced from choice, it is a physical concept; it becomes irrelevant whether cost is measured before, at the moment of, or after actual commitment. In the Smithian model, the cost of a beaver is two deer, and this holds so long as the postulated physical relationships hold; there is no point in distinguishing *ex ante* and *ex post* measurements. Because of the technological or physical nature of cost, derived from the transformation function in commodity space, the alternatives facing the actor can be "costed" by an external observer. There is no need for the observer to psychoanalyze the hunter in Smith's model. And the problem of dating does not arise in the objective definition implicit in the predictive theory. On the other hand, cost must be precisely dated in any theory of genuine choice because it is tied to the moment of choice as such. Before choice, cost exists as a subjective experience. After choice, cost vanishes in this sense. What happens to the chooser after he has chosen remains to be considered.

Choice-Influencing and Choice-Influenced Cost

The six attributes of cost listed above are relevant to any particular choice. If cost is to be influential in affecting *that* choice, it must be defined in terms of these attributes. Nonetheless, we must also recognize that choice has consequences: things happen as a result of decisions. Having committed himself to one course of action rather than another and having presumably made some rational estimation of the costs that this would embody, the individual "suffers" the consequences. He may not regret his prior decision, but, at the same time, he may undergo "pain" or "sacrifice" when he is required to reduce his utility levels. Whether or not choices were rightly or wrongly made has little direct relevance to the existence of this choice-influenced "cost."

It is this "cost" consequent to choice which helps to create a part of the confusion between cost in the predictive theory and cost in the logic of choice. That which happens after choice is made is what economists seem to be talking about when they draw their cost curves on the blackboards and what accountants seem to be concerning themselves with. It is necessary that this choice-influenced "cost" be more thoroughly examined.

If we bend linguistic principle to accommodate orthodox usage here, it seems best to allow the word "cost" to be used in these two quite separate senses within any theory of choice, while continuing to employ this same term in its single usage in the predictive theory of economic behavior. Hence, we have both "choice-influencing cost" and "choice-influenced cost" within the theory of choice and defined in *utility space,* and we have "objective cost," defined strictly in the commodity space of the predictive theory. Let us now neglect the objective cost of the predictive science and concentrate on choice-influencing and choice-influenced cost. Every choice involves both of these. First, there is the genuine obstacle to choice, the opportunity cost that was central to the thoughts of those economists whose contributions were summarized in Chapter 2. Second, there are the utility losses that are always consequent to choice having been made, whether these be suffered by the chooser or by third parties and whether there may or may not be objectively measurable surrogates for these losses, e.g., payouts. These losses are the result of decision and never its cause. In the one case, cost inhibits choice; in the other, cost results from choice. These concepts of cost can be discussed more fully in connection with several of the familiar, but ultimately misleading distinctions.

Opportunity Cost and Real Cost

Strictly speaking, only choice-influencing cost represents an evaluation of sacrificed "opportunities." It might therefore be reasonable to limit the term *opportunity cost* to this conception and to invent other descriptive appellations to refer both to choice-influenced cost in a logic of choice and to the objective cost of the predictive theory. In a more general sense, however, any one of the three conceptions may be meaningfully treated in opportunity-cost terms. In the orthodox price-theory conception where cost is measured objectively by money outlays, it is helpful, for explanatory purposes, to equate these outlays to the values that members of society place on the alternate end products that might have been produced by the same outlays differently directed. In a certain ambiguous sense, therefore, cost here does reflect "opportunities lost." But it is noteworthy that the "opportunities lost" in this context more accurately reflect the value of potential alternatives as judged by others rather than by the chooser himself.

The notion of "opportunities lost" can also be applied to the results of choice, or to choice-influenced cost. Here the concept is tied to the choice and the opportunities represent those things that "might have been," as these are viewed after decision has been made. Given this hindsight, alternatives can be viewed differently than they were viewed before a commitment was made. Within a before-choice, or choice-influencing context, the opportunities lost are those that "might be," as considered and evaluated at the moment of choice itself and as reflected in the presently anticipated value of utility losses expected to be incurred. Within the post-choice or choice-influenced context, by comparison, the opportunities lost are those that might have been enjoyed, as these are reflected in experienced utility losses or sacrifices. There can be an important psychological difference in the utility losses involved in choice-influencing and in choice-influenced cost. At the moment of choice itself, cost is the chooser's evaluation of the anticipated enjoyments that he must give up once commitment is made; it is also that which he can avoid by choosing another alternative. Cost in this setting must be and remain a purely mental event. The chooser's utility is reduced only in the sense that it is functionally dependent on *expected* utility in post-decision time periods. After the choice is made, cost may still reflect the evaluation of enjoyments that were sacrificed and cost remains a mental event, but there is more to it than this. Among the experiences that might have been avoided may be those requiring an explicit submission to pain, to suffering, to deprivation, in some physically relevant meaning of the terms. Having made a charge-account commitment, the buyer must pay his bills when they come due. Despite his possibly rational anticipation of this cost at the moment of choice, he still suffers pain when these bills must be met. This purely physical exposure to negative choice-determined effects enters into his subjective evaluation of the alternative that might have been. In a certain sense, therefore, the nature of cost is different in the choice-influencing and the choice-influenced contexts, although both remain in utility space.

So long as we treat cost in either a cost-influencing or a choice-influenced sense, that is to say, so long as we remain with the theory of choice itself, we are closer to the classical notion of real cost than is the neoclassical conception. Either as an obstacle to choice or as an undesirable consequence of choice, cost represents utility loss. In relatively sharp contrast, when cost is divorced from the choice process, as in the neoclassical predictive setting, there is nothing "real" about it. No pain, suffering, or utility loss is involved. This seems to have been the basis for Knight's conceptual distinction between opportunity cost and real cost which led him to say that ". . . all references to 'sacrifices' (should be) simply omitted."[1]

The Subjectivity of Sunk Costs

I have referred to cost in any logic of choice as "subjective" and to cost in any predictive science as "objective." In a preliminary discussion in another volume,[2] I employed the subjective-objective terminology ambiguously, because I failed at that time to distinguish the separate dimensions of cost within these related but quite different settings. Cost in the predictive models of economics must be objective. If cost is introduced into a logic of choice, however, it is obviously subjective. This has been repeatedly emphasized by some of the LSE scholars whose works were mentioned earlier, and notably by G. F. Thirlby.

The consequences of choice, the results of decision, enter the individual's experiences as subjectively valued events, even though, as noted, there may also be physical repercussions to the decision. If a commitment is made and things happen, such happenings affect the individual's utility—quite independently of the fact that they cannot be avoided. The individual suffers utility loss as a consequence of a prior decision even if, on balance, the decision was itself fully rational. This suffering is a subjective event whether it be regrets at what might have been or pain at what is. Strictly speaking, only this subjective choice-determined cost squares fully with the economist's concept of "sunk cost" or with Jevons' "bygones." Since choice has been made, this cost is irrelevant excepting insofar as the experience may modify anticipations about choice alternatives in the future.

1. F. H. Knight, "A Suggestion for Simplifying the Statement of the General Theory of Price," *Journal of Political Economy,* XXXVI (June 1928), 355.
2. See my "Public Debt, Cost Theory, and the Fiscal Illusion," in *Public Debt and Future Generations,* James M. Ferguson (ed.) (Chapel Hill: University of North Carolina Press, 1964), pp. 150–62.

In this choice-influenced sense, cost is related to choice *ex post*, but it is not personally tied to the chooser or decision-maker. This is an important distinction that has contributed its own share in the general cost-theory confusion. As we noted earlier in connection with the first-listed attribute of choice-influencing cost, the opportunity cost must be borne by the decision-taker himself if choice is to be affected at all. Indeed, in this context, cost can be borne *only* by the chooser; the whole notion becomes meaningless otherwise. By contrast, the consequences of choice—the utility losses suffered as a result of a decision—need not be endured only by the chooser. Because these consequences are always realized *after* choice, the chooser himself may be considered a different person once the consequences of choice are realized. Even when this is neglected, however, there remains no formal connection between the person taking a decision and the person or persons who suffer utility losses as a result. Those who "bear the burden"—even though bearing this burden is a subjective experience—need not be those who undergo the "agony of choosing."

Cost and Equilibrium

Given presumably objective data drawn from nonutility space, neoclassical economics makes predictions about properties of the equilibrium relationships that will tend to be established behaviorally by participants in the market-interaction process. To what extent does the equilibrium emphasis allow for some reconciliation between the two cost conceptions, between the objective cost of the predictive science and the purely subjective cost in the logic of choice? Do objectively measurable outlays reflect foregone opportunities only under conditions of full equilibrium?

If the whole economy is not operating at full competitive equilibrium, profits-losses may occur and, hence, observed outlays cannot be taken to reflect foregone opportunities of the actual decision-takers in any general setting. In full equilibrium, on the other hand, observed outlays directly represent the maximum contribution of resources in different uses. Therefore, to the extent that decision-takers behave economically, the observed outlays reflect genuine "opportunity costs," even if somewhat indirectly. The apparent reconciliation here verges on the tautological, however, since the whole purpose of the economic theory in which cost is relevant is to demonstrate how choices made in nonequilibrium settings will generate shifts toward equilibrium. And choices in disequilibrium must be informed by opportunity costs that cannot, even indirectly, be represented by measured outlays. In disequilibrium, the opportunity costs involved in taking the "wrong" decision must include the profits foregone in the rejection of the alternative course of action.

Marginalism provides only a partial rescue here. If an individual behaves economically, and if no profit opportunities exist *elsewhere* in the whole system, and if all decisions can and must be made marginally, the marginal-cost derivation of orthodox theory can be taken to represent the genuine "opportunity cost" of an output decision. This means that all choices are made at equilibrium in the short-term planning context where output decisions within the firm are conceptually divorced from the rest of the economy. It is essential, however, for each of the qualifying conditions to be satisfied if measured marginal cost is to be employed as an objective representation of the subjective element that actually enters the individual's choice calculus.

If, on the other hand, the individual incorporates nonpecuniary or noneconomic considerations in his decision, if there are profits to be secured elsewhere than in the activity in question, if discrete rather than marginal adjustments are possible, then objectively measured marginal outlay is not a veritable expression of genuine opportunity cost, because these "ifs" may represent inhibitions upon choice behavior which are not susceptible to objective measurement.

There is necessarily a close correlation between the relevance of objectively measured costs for a theory of choice in either long-term or short-term equilibrium and the presence or absence of uncertainty. In the face of uncertainty, the evaluation of alternatives by the actual decision-taker may differ from the evaluations of any external observer, even if the qualifying conditions are met. The inherent subjectivity of cost in any theory of choice reasserts itself here.

The equilibrium concepts introduced in this section up to this point are those of the predictive neoclassical theory. This implies that descriptions of equilibrium take the form of objectively defined relationships among variables in nonutility dimensions. Prices must bear specific relationships to costs. If we are content to remain within a more general, but ultimately nonpredictive and purely logical theory of economic choice, the concept of equilibrium may be modified. The equilibrium of the "subjectivist economics" espoused by Hayek is described behaviorally. It is attained when the plans of participants in the economic interaction process are mutually satisfied. Although prices continue in this equilibrium to bear some relationship to costs, such costs carry no objective meaning and cannot, therefore, be employed as criteria for determining prices in some welfare or efficiency sense.

4. The Cost of Public Goods

The predictive science of economics postulates that men behave "economically." They act so as to minimize "cost" in some objectively identifiable sense. By a curious inversion, economists have applied the postulate of behavior that has proved helpful in deriving positive predictions as a *norm* in a theory of choice. Throughout applied economics, the theory of economic policy, or welfare economics, we find norms that are defined in terms of specified relationships between "costs" and "prices," relationships that embody conceptually measurable objective magnitudes. In effect, though perhaps inadvertently, the applied economist and the welfare theorist alike accept the behavior of *Homo economicus* as a value criterion. In their zeal to apply economic theory not to an analysis of institutional interactions but to real choice, they indirectly propose that decision-takers, singly or in the aggregate, *should* minimize objectively measurable outlays. This error is fundamental, and it extends from the estimation of national income to the economics of defense.[1]

Only a few of the many applications can be discussed in detail here, but these will perhaps be sufficient to indicate the importance of the methodological distinctions that I have emphasized. Somewhat arbitrarily I shall limit my discussion to three separate areas. In this chapter, I shall examine the various problems that arise when the concept of "cost" is applied to public or collective goods. A discussion of some of the difficulties in Pigovian welfare economics and in nonmarket decision-making follows this.

1. For a critical discussion of the measurement of national product which is grounded on analysis that is related to, although quite different from, the analysis developed here, see S. H. Frankel, *The Economic Impact on Under-Developed Societies* (Cambridge: Harvard University Press, 1953), esp. Chapter III.

The Theory of Tax Incidence

The theory of tax incidence commands a lion's share of attention in neoclassical public finance, especially among English-language scholars. A cursory examination of this literature suggests that the aim is to answer the questions: Who pays for public goods and services? Who bears the final burden of payment under specified tax instruments? How does the allocation of "cost" or "burden" differ under different taxes?

The two words "cost" and "burden" seem to be used almost interchangeably. The presumed objectivity of these magnitudes has more or less been taken for granted. The revenues collected by the treasury can, after all, be counted. Someone must be subjected to this "cost"; someone must release command over purchasing power which represents, in its turn, real resources. Certain taxes generate "excess burdens" over and above the actual revenue collections, but these, too, are objectively quantifiable, at least conceptually. There has been little or no attention paid to the possible relationship between taxes as the costs of public goods and taxes in choices for public goods.

Shifting and incidence analysis examines the choice behavior of individuals and firms, but this is not the choice behavior that involves either the financing of public goods or the selection among taxing alternatives. The individual or firm is assumed to be subjected to an imposed change in the alternatives of *private* or *market* choice. Here, taxes can affect cost in a choice-influencing context, and, indeed, incidence theory would be empty if this were not the case. Consider the familiar benchmark, the lump-sum tax. No shifting takes place here; incidence is not in question. But surely there is a "cost" of public goods borne by individuals, and "choice" must be made. Contrast this with an excise tax, say, on liquor. Here the tax, if shifted by the seller, modifies the alternatives that the prospective buyer confronts, because the "cost" of buying liquor increases. It is here that the predictive or positive theory is at its strongest. Since both the object of consumption and the numeraire can be readily identified as "goods" in the individual's utility function and since, before the tax, the individual's rates of purchase for all "goods" could be assumed to be in equilibrium, the objectively measurable increase in cost, as reflected in the tax-induced price rise, can be seen as representative of the increase in subjective cost that actually inhibits consumer choice for the taxed commodity. It is erroneous, however, to relate the tax-induced increase in a consumption-goods price—hence, in its "cost" to the buyer—with the wholly different "cost" of the public good which the tax revenues somehow represent. This leads us back to the initial questions. As traditionally developed, does incidence theory really aim at locating the cost of public goods? Orthodox tax-shifting and incidence analysis is concerned almost exclusively with tax-induced changes in the costs of undertaking *private* activities of production, investment, and consumption and with predictions of the effects of such changes on behavior.

If the analysis yields no information about the costs of public goods, what value does it have for anyone? If the economist can with confidence trace the full effects of a tax, he is able, presumably, to array this tax against others on some postulated scale of equity or efficiency. In this task, he conceives his role as that of advising the decision-maker, hence indirectly influencing the choice that is made among tax instruments. This seems straightforward enough until the sometimes weird results of presuming the objective measurability of cost are recognized. In assessing the consequences—or predicted consequences—of a tax levy, is the economist seeking to determine the measurable changes in the values of empirically descriptive variables such as prices, quantities, and employment levels? Or is he seeking to determine the individuals' evaluations of these changes?

Consider a simple example. Suppose that the pre-tax price of liquor is $10 per bottle and that an individual is observed to purchase 10 bottles per year for a total outlay of $100. A specific excise tax of $1 is imposed; the retail price is observed to rise by the full amount of the tax to $11; and the individual's annual rate of purchase falls to 9 bottles, for an annual outlay of $99. Assuming a linear demand curve over the relevant range, the economist says that the "burden" of the tax is computed at $9.50, with $9 being channeled through to the treasury and 50¢ being an "excess burden." On familiar grounds, the individual is simply assumed to "prefer" a lump-sum tax that would require him to pay only $9. On "welfare" principles, therefore, the economist suggests the desirability of the lump-sum tax as a substitute for the excise tax.[2] To reach this conclusion, the economist must assume that the taxpayer is ex-

---

2. I am not concerned here with various modern qualifications on this proposition, all of which derive from some version of second-best limitations. My criticism holds even if all of the welfare conditions are fully satisfied elsewhere in the system.

clusively interested in the post-tax changes in his position and that he is in-different among tax instruments otherwise. But there are obviously many reasons why the taxpayer may not evaluate alternative tax instruments in the same way that the applied welfare economist evaluates them. The taxpayer might, in the first place, prefer to suffer the higher measurable cost imposed by the excise tax because of the wider range of personal options that this form of tax allows. This option feature may well outweigh the excess burden. In the second place, the taxpayer may prefer the excise tax on liquor for sumptuary reasons even though he knows that he, too, bears an excess bur-den. The tax-induced reduction in liquor purchases by others may be more than enough to modify the relative standing of this tax on his preference scale.[3]

Even if the applied economist is uninterested in the evaluations of taxpay-ers in any sense relevant to their possible participation in fiscal choice and relies instead on an externally derived "social welfare function" in establish-ing his array of tax instruments, the difficulties raised above do not disap-pear. He would be hard put to defend the objectively measurable "cost" emerging from the orthodox tax-shifting analysis as a criterion for arraying tax devices if such a "cost" did not in some way relate to individuals' own reactions and evaluations.

Costs and Fiscal Decision-Making: The Democratic Model

What are the "costs" of public goods in the genuine opportunity-cost, or *choice-influencing,* sense? This question itself ties costs directly to choice and immediately requires some identification of the choosing agent. The connec-tion between the political decision structure and public finance cannot be avoided. Traditional incidence theory is presumed useful in providing bases for better informed choices of tax instruments. But it is not possible to dis-

3. In an earlier work, I have tried to relate the effects of different fiscal instruments on the individual's behavior in fiscal process. See my *Public Finance in Democratic Process* (Chapel Hill: University of North Carolina Press, 1967). See also Charles Goetz, "Tax Pref-erences in a Collective Decision-Making Context" (Unpublished Ph.D. dissertation, Al-derman Library, University of Virginia, 1964).

cuss these choices without identifying the choice-maker. Who decides? The answer depends on the way in which political decisions get made. This is obvious enough, but what is so often overlooked is that "costs" vary significantly over the many different decision structures.

Let us consider first a simplified collective-decision model, which we can associate with de Viti de Marco. Here the individual who makes the fiscal decision is both the prospective consumer-beneficiary of public goods and the prospective taxpayer. This model has been variously called "individualistic," "cooperative," and "democratic" by different scholars. The great advantage of this model is that the choice within it closely resembles that made by the individual in his market behavior. He chooses to tax himself in order to secure the benefits of the public good. What does the individual forego in making a choice? In making a choice, the individual foregoes the possibility of avoiding the actual tax outlay; and consequently he foregoes the enjoyment of those goods which might have been purchased with this predicted outlay. The subjective value placed on these alternative goods is a relevant *choice-influencing* cost. This much seems apparent, but is there any reason for thinking that the money outlay, even if this could be accurately predicted, reflects the subjective barrier to the individual's decision?

As our earlier analysis indicated, for this anticipated outlay to measure, even indirectly, the subjective cost, it must be assumed that no profit opportunities exist elsewhere in the economy, *including the public sector*. But there is an additional complication that must also be recognized, one that was mentioned earlier but not discussed in detail. Collective goods are not purchased individually. Each person cannot adjust his own desired purchases; all must accept the *same* outcome. At best, the tax side of a fiscal decision is a vector, the components of which represent the levies on *each* member of the group. Consider, then, the decision calculus of the person who participates in such "democratic" fiscal choice. He "votes for" an outlay on a public good that is to be shared by all members of the community. What are the costs that will influence this choice? What are the genuinely foregone alternatives that he rejects? By not approving the proposed budgetary outlay, the individual's own tax outlay can be avoided, and, under the rigidly restrictive assumptions about the absence of profits elsewhere, this anticipated outlay can be taken to reflect indirectly at least one part of cost. In rejecting the budgetary proposal, however, the individual also avoids, or chooses to avoid, all other consequences of the collective decision. On the cost side, these anticipated consequences are the tax payments made by *others* than the particular individual whose choice we are examining. If he positively evaluates the foregone enjoyments that others might purchase with these outlays, some cost element emerges. Choice-influencing cost as an obstacle to the individual's approval of a public-goods decision can be measured by his own expected share in the tax payments only in the extreme case where he places no value at all on the relief of others from "suffering."

If this applies for one participant in a group choice, it must apply to all. Hence, the total tax payment that is anticipated, measured in money terms, may be a grossly inaccurate estimate of the "social" cost of the budgetary outlay that is considered. The choice-influencing cost to each participant, and hence to all participants in some additive sense, may far exceed the estimate produced by the simple summation of individual shares.

This does not imply that the group-decision aspects are limited to the cost side. For precisely the same reasons, the individual will reckon the prospective benefits from a proposed public-goods outlay to include not only those that he expects to secure privately and individually, but also the value that he places on the anticipated benefits flows to others as their share in the commonly consumed good. Just as with the cost side, any measure of anticipated benefits derived from a simple summation of separate shares is likely to be grossly in error.

A recognition of these points suggests the limited relevance of modern cost-benefit analysis, which seems aimed at providing some measures of genuine "social" costs and benefits from proposed projects. The assumption that anticipated costs, as measured, will equal anticipated benefits, as measured, implies that the group should somehow be on a margin of indifference in its collective or "social" choice for or against the project. As we have demonstrated, however, there is not the remotest reason for making any such inference, even apart from the important distributional issues that have not yet been raised at all. If the proposed tax should be levied equally on all persons and the proposed benefits shared equally, there would still be no presumption that a measured cost-benefit ratio of unity should imply indifference in group-choice.

Costs and Decision-Making:
The Authoritarian Model

Choice-influencing costs of public goods differ with the location of effective decision-making power in the collectivity. Even in the most naive of democratic models in which the decision-maker is assumed to be both the prospective taxpayer and the prospective beneficiary in some "representative" sense, genuine opportunity costs must include the individual's evaluation of enjoyments foregone by others. The fact of *collective* decision requires this. It is clear that when more complex models of decision-making are introduced, this nonpersonal aspect of costs becomes more significant. To illustrate this, we may shift attention to the nondemocratic extreme of the spectrum and examine an authoritarian decision-structure.

Assume that all decisions for the collectivity are made by a single person who has dictatorial powers. Limiting analysis to public finance, what are the choice-influencing costs in such a setting? What are the obstacles to the dictator's decision on the levy of a tax to finance a specific governmental outlay? In the limit, he will not personally bear any share of the prospective tax to be imposed. The "costs" that might be avoided by a decision not to impose the tax are, therefore, exclusively represented in the dictator's evaluation of the enjoyments which others than himself might secure in the absence of the tax. In such a decision context as this, it seems almost meaningless to use anticipated outlay or payment as an indirect representation of that cost which influences choice. As mentioned above, cost-benefit analysis may produce wildly inaccurate estimates even in the most unsophisticated of democratic models, because the collective aspects of both costs and benefits are ignored. The results of such analysis are not, however, without some relevance. By contrast, cost-benefit analysis of the orthodox variety when applied to the authoritarian model becomes absurd since *no part* of the anticipated outlay, as measured, is expected to be borne by the man who makes the choice.

Costs and Decision-Making: Mixed Models

In any real-world political setting, collective decisions are made through institutional processes that usually reflect some mixture of the purely democratic and the purely authoritarian models. Most individuals participate, directly or indirectly, in the formation of group decisions, but some persons participate more fully than others. That is to say, the effectiveness with which particular individuals and groups influence decision-making is widely variable. In such a setting, the costs that influence the choice calculus of an individual participant depend, first, on his own personalized or individualized share in an anticipated payment or outlay and his evaluation of this outlay in terms of his own foregone enjoyments. In addition, he must evaluate the enjoyments that he thinks others must forego as they are subjected to the taxing process. Only if each participant in the group-decision process should evaluate the foregone enjoyments of all others as equally important with his own would the *distribution* of the anticipated tax payments make no difference in the "costs," as these influence or modify decisions. If *each* individual, no matter what his power over collective decisions, should subjectively value the prospective tax dollar paid by *each* other person equally with his own, then *neither* the distribution of decision-making power *nor* the distribution of tax shares would modify the costs which are the obstacles to choice. In such a limiting case, orthodox cost-benefit measurements might be reasonably accurate representations of choice-influencing costs and benefits. Merely the requirements of such a model are sufficient to indicate its manifest absurdity.[4]

Defenders of cost-benefit estimation may respond here by stating that collective decisions, however and by whomever made, *should* be guided by the project comparisons that the estimates reveal. The purpose of cost-benefit analysis, this argument suggests, is not that of ascertaining genuine oppor-

---

4. It is interesting to note that sophisticated cost-benefit analysts recognize the relevance of the distribution of tax shares (or benefit shares), while at the same time they fail to recognize the relevance of the distribution of decision-making power. The oversight of this second distributional effect stems, of course, from the paradigm in which "costs" exist as objectively quantifiable magnitudes, unrelated to the choice process. Among the applied welfare economists who have examined the methodology of cost-benefit analysis, only Roland N. McKean seems to be aware that a problem so much as exists here. See his paper, "The Use of Shadow Prices," in Samuel B. Chase, Jr. (ed.), *Problems in Public Expenditure Analysis* (Washington, D.C.: Brookings Institution, 1968), pp. 33–65. For a specific discussion of the importance of the distribution of tax or benefit shares, see the paper by Burton A. Weisbrod, "Income Redistribution Effects and Benefit-Cost Analysis," pp. 177–208 in the same volume.

tunity costs in a choice-influencing context, but rather that of laying down rules for choice. But why should objectively measurable costs be taken to reflect "social cost" under any reasonable meaning of this term? The evaluations of individuals should be relevant in any attempt to derive normative statements, but these evaluations bear little direct relationship to measured outlays for the several reasons noted, the most important of which are, of course, distributional.

At this point, the defender of cost-benefit orthodoxy may reject the implied limitation of his estimation procedure to objectively measurable cost and benefit streams. He may suggest including in predicted costs and benefits some estimates for subjectively valued, but objectively immeasurable, characteristics of alternatives. With this step, however, the whole analysis is subtly converted from one that can claim potential agreement among competent scientists to one that is purely subjective, not to the actual decision-makers, but to the economist who offers his normative advice. The cost-benefit expert cannot have it both ways. He cannot claim "scientific" precision for his estimates unless he restricts himself rigidly to objectively observable magnitudes. But if he does this, he cannot claim that his estimates reflect reasonable norms upon which "social" choices should be based.

The Choice Among Projects

To this point, attention has been limited to the cost side of a possible decision to impose a tax for the purpose of financing a specific government project. This particular choice involves a cost, but one that is quite different from that which arises when different choices are considered. One of these is the selection of one from among many public projects. Here the choice-influencing cost will be quite different from that involved in the decision to impose the tax. To each particular decision there is attached a unique opportunity cost and this depends on the particular characteristics of the decision.

Economists have often noted that the genuine opportunity costs of projects undertaken during periods of massive unemployment are nonexistent. Care must be taken, however, to specify the precise meaning of this conclusion and to examine the particulars of the decision in question. First, consider the decision as to whether or not to issue new currency to finance any new spending, public or private, during a period of deep depression. The alternatives are, first, those of doing nothing about the deficiency in aggregate demand and, second, financing new spending from taxation or public loans. Since, by assumption, unemployed resources are available, the issue of currency promises to generate no inflationary pressures. To the decision-maker who is properly informed, there are no "real costs," in the sense of enjoyments to be foregone either by himself or others. Since either of the alternative courses of action, even if the identical benefits stream is promised, will impose such real costs, he will tend to choose currency issue. For this choice, it is correct to say that there is, or should be, no cost obstacle. If, however, despite the presence of unemployed resources, taxation is selected as the financing device, the choice here necessarily involves a cost. The alternative uses to which money paid out in taxes might be put are foregone by the decision-maker and others once taxation is decided upon; and these foregone alternatives must be evaluated at the time of choice. The existence of unemployment may cause even these choice-influencing costs to be low relative to the choice-influencing benefits of the new spending, but there is no denying that "real costs" exist.

The financing choice, that which is involved in a potential decision to issue currency or to finance new spending through other means, must be sharply distinguished from the spending choice, which arises when a selection among projects must be made. There is, first, the choice between using the funds to expand private-sector or public-sector spending. The choice of a public-sector project involves an opportunity cost that is represented in the anticipated foregone enjoyments from the possible expansions in private-sector spending that might be generated by the same funds. Once the option has been made for a public-sector project, still another choice must be confronted, and this also involves a choice-influencing cost, an obstacle to decision. Once currency has been issued, and the decision has been made to expand public-sector spending, the choice among separate public employments of the funds must be faced. The choice-influencing cost of the new post office building is the subjective value that the decision-maker places on the new school building that might be constructed instead. The familiar statement, "The post offices built during the 1930's cost very little in terms of sacrificed alternatives" tends to be misleading. These projects did involve genuine opportunity costs to the decision-makers, and these were represented as the prospective values of other public and private projects that were never undertaken. The issue of currency, to the extent that this was carried out in the conditions of the 1930's, was the choice that should have cost very little in terms of sacrificed alternatives.

The Costs of Debt-Financed Public Goods

Nowhere has the elemental confusion in cost theory been more in evidence than in the sometimes acrimonious discussion of public-debt incidence. Indeed, it was precisely through my own involvement in the modern debt-burden controversy and my subsequent attempt to reconcile my notions with those of respected fellow economists that my attention was directed to cost theory.[5] The debt-burden problem illustrates the necessity of distinguishing between choice-influencing and choice-influenced cost on the one hand, and the necessity of relating cost directly to choice on the other.

Consider, first, the view that was very widely held by sophisticated economists prior to 1958. It was alleged that the "real burden" of debt-financed public goods, the genuine opportunity costs, must be experienced during the time period when the real resources were actually used. In the case of the debts of World War II, the steel was used to make guns in 1943 and not in some later period. It seemed manifest nonsense, a violation of the most elementary opportunity-cost reasoning, to claim that public-debt burden was "shifted to future generations."

As difficult as it may seem in 1969 to hold such a view (despite its continued espousal in nonsophisticated textbook discussion), orthodox opportunity-cost reasoning, which measures real costs in terms of real resources objectively quantified and which concentrates on costs *independently* of the particulars of decision, leads quite logically to this conception. *Who* gives up command over the real resources that are secured for public use under debt financing? The obvious answer is those who purchase the debt instruments from the treasury. These bond purchasers are not at all concerned about the decision to issue debt; their choice is simply whether to purchase debt or to

---

5. In my early book, my ideas on cost were confused. See my *Public Principles of Public Debt* (Homewood, Ill.: Richard D. Irwin, 1958). Somewhat later, in response to critics, I traced the differences in debt theory to cost-theory confusions. My contribution, along with other papers, is contained in James M. Ferguson (ed.), *Public Debt and Future Generations* (Chapel Hill: University of North Carolina Press, 1964).

purchase privately available investment or consumption goods. These bond purchasers surely do not participate in the fiscal choice as such. They cannot be said to bear the "cost" of the public goods that the debt issue finances. To locate the genuine cost of public goods, a cost which influences fiscal choice, we must look at the fiscal alternatives. What is avoided if debt is not issued and the public goods not provided?

If public debt is not created, if bonds are not marketed, the decision-maker, along with others in the collectivity, avoids the necessity of servicing and amortizing the debt in *future* periods. The costs of debt issue, in the way that they may influence a decision among fiscal alternatives, must be reflected in the decision-maker's subjective evaluation of these subsequent outlays. In the choice-influencing sense, these costs are concentrated in the moment of choice and not in the later periods during which the actual outlays must be made. But the choice-influencing, subjective costs exist only because of the decision-maker's recognition that it will be necessary to make future-period outlays. The concentration of choice-influencing cost in the moment of decision arises from the simple fact that a decision is made; this cost has no relationship whatsoever to and is not influenced by the fact that resources are used up in the initial period.

The choice-influenced costs of debt-financed projects, the losses in utility as a result of choice, are borne exclusively in periods subsequent to decision. These actual payments, which may also be measured in money, may reduce the utilities of others than those who participate in the decision. In one sense, this burden of debt is always deadweight, and its location in time has no relationship whatever to the time period during which the public projects yield their benefits.

Some of the contributors to the modern discussion of public-debt theory have acknowledged that, by comparison with tax-financing, debt issue does impose a relative "burden on future generations." They reach this conclusion, however, because debt-financing is alleged to reduce private capital formation to a relatively greater degree than tax-financing. Hence, "future generations" inherit a somewhat smaller capital stock under current public-debt financing than they would under current tax-financing for similar public outlays. This line of argument, which can be associated with Vickrey and Modigliani,[6] is also based on the failure to relate cost to choice. Whether or

---

6. See their contributions in Ferguson, op. cit. A similar error is made by Feldstein and

not private capital formation is or is not relatively reduced by debt-financing is irrelevant to the location of debt burden in periods subsequent to choice. Even should all funds for the purchase of bonds be drawn from current consumption, the subjective costs of debt issue still consist in the decision-maker's evaluation of the enjoyments that must be foregone, by himself and by others, in future periods when the outlays for servicing and amortization must be made. The decision of a prospective *bond purchaser* is, of course, relevant to the rate of private capital formation, but this is not the same decision as that of the prospective *bond seller*. If the bond purchaser draws down private investment, he does impose a "burden" on his heirs in future periods, and the recognition of this will be the obstacle to his choice. If he draws down current consumption, no such burden is imposed. But the point to be emphasized here is that his choice is quite a separate and different one from that made by the debt issuer. The emphasis on the capital-formation aspects of public debt seems to arise from a confusion of the results of not one, but two decisions, and the calculus of not one, but two sets of decision-makers.

Ricardo's Equivalence Theorem

Ricardo advanced the theorem that a rational person should be indifferent between the levy of an extraordinary tax and the issue of a public loan of equal value. In his model, he assumed that the individual held an infinitely

---

endorsed by Prest and Turvey in their review of cost-benefit analysis. In Feldstein's view, the cost of a project depends, in part, on whether or not the funds are withdrawn from current consumption or from investment. However, to the extent that cost-benefit measurements are helpful at all, the persons from whom funds are secured, presumably in this case through taxes, must be assumed to be in equilibrium between consumption and investment outlays. In this case, the utilities per dollar's worth have been equalized at the margin. As suggested earlier, unless such full equilibrium is assumed, the whole approach, which is limited at best, becomes worthless. See M. S. Feldstein, "Opportunity Cost Calculations in Cost-Benefit Analysis," *Public Finance*, XIX (1964), 126, as cited in A. R. Prest and R. Turvey, "Cost-Benefit Analysis: A Survey," *Economic Journal*, LXXV (December 1965), 686–87.

Interestingly enough, Davenport seems to have indirectly warned against this error a half-century ago. He stressed that the cost to a borrower (that which he must give up in order to secure funds) has no direct relationship to the cost to the lender (that which he must give up when he makes a consumption-saving decision). Two distinct choices are involved and hence two costs. See H. J. Davenport, *Value and Distribution* (Chicago: University of Chicago Press, 1908), p. 260.

long time horizon and that capital markets were perfect in the sense that the individual could borrow at the same rate as the collectivity. Under such conditions, the individual could without cost transform one of these two fiscal alternatives into the other via transactions in the capital market. It follows that he should be indifferent between them.

As such, the analysis is elementary and obvious. But a similar analysis could be extended to any act of individual choice. If, for example, the individual is informed that he may always exchange one orange for one apple through the market, he will be indifferent between a gift of an orange and an apple because of the possibility of costless transformation. This does not imply, however, that one orange will be equal to one apple in the individual's subjective evaluation. The latter equality emerges only if the individual is allowed to adjust quantities bought and sold to a point where behavioral equilibrium is fully attained. In isolated, nonequilibrium situations, no such subjective-valuation equality may be presumed. Hence, as applied to the public-loan–taxation alternatives, the individual remains indifferent because he can make the costless transformation, not because the two alternatives are of equal value in his subjective consideration of them.

The recognition of this simple point suggests that the conversion of the public-loan alternative to a present-value equivalent may not accurately measure, or represent, the genuine choice-influencing cost that the debt issue embodies. If the individual is observed to opt for the public-debt alternative, it is an indication that its cost is *below* that of the tax alternative, which is defined to be equal to the present value of future debt-service and amortization charges. It cannot be inferred that the choice of the individual is marginal. The choice-influencing opportunity costs, the subjective evaluation of the sacrifice of future-period enjoyments, may be substantially below the figure represented by the current capitalized value of the necessary payment obligations. Only if it is presumed that the individual has fully adjusted his spending-saving patterns so as to bring his own rate of time discount into equality with the market rate, can it be alleged that the individual should be on a subjective margin of indifference between the two fiscal instruments. Indeed, it is precisely the differences among the subjective valuations of equal present-value instruments with differing time dimensions that causes the individual to behave so as to move toward full equilibrium. From a methodological point of view, it is surely illegitimate to derive implications for choice among equal present-value instruments, assets or liabilities, from the characteristics of the equilibrium toward which such choice behavior aims.

Tax Capitalization

The Ricardian theorem is related to a separate fiscal-theory application that consistent cost theory may clarify. What, precisely, do fiscal theorists mean when they say that a tax may be fully capitalized under certain conditions? The arithmetic is straightforward: the present value of the asset subjected to a newly imposed tax is written down to reflect the weight of expected future taxes as charges against income. A purchaser of the asset, after the moment of capitalization, will not bear any part of the tax burden; this will rest exclusively on the owner of the asset at the time of imposition.

There is nothing wrong in this summary statement of the orthodox analysis provided that the conditions where capitalization can occur are carefully specified. The presumption is often made, however, that the "burden" of the tax is experienced, subjectively, *only* in the period when the asset's capital value is written down and that no further sacrifice of utility is involved. This is based on elementary confusion. The moment of capitalization corresponds to the moment of choice in our earlier discussion of cost, and it may clarify the analysis to think of an asset owner's making a choice which involves giving up, either in taxation or in some other form, a claim to a part of the asset's future income stream. There will be a choice-influencing opportunity cost here, a purely subjective evaluation of the alternatives that must be foregone by the fact of the abandonment of future-period claims to income. However, just as with debt issue, this subjective cost arises only because of the expectation that, in future periods, some payment must be made from income, that some potential enjoyment from the use of income must be foregone. Once the choice is made and the tax or other claim against the asset's income is imposed, consequences follow, and these include the contracted necessity of making the required payments. These become the *choice-influenced* costs of the decision taken earlier, and these can be measured objectively as well as evaluated subjectively. The owner of the asset experiences utility losses in such later periods. These cannot be eliminated by the process of capitalization since, in fact, the anticipation of these future-period utility losses is the only basis for the subjective costs experienced at the moment of choice or of capitalization.

There has been here some confusion between the transfer of burden among asset owners and the temporal location of this burden. Capitalization concentrates the tax burden on the owner of an asset at the moment of the initial levy. But "at the moment" refers to the ownership pattern, not to the tax burden. Even if the owner should sell the asset immediately after full capitalization, he will still experience the choice-influenced costs in subsequent time periods.

In tax capitalization, as in ordinary economic choice, there are two costs, not one, and it is necessary to keep these distinct. Fully analogous to the choice-influencing cost of any decision, there is the purely subjective realization that future income streams are reduced. This is experienced in the sensation of evaluating the future enjoyment of opportunities that have suddenly been foreclosed. Analogous to choice-influenced cost, there is the experienced utility loss that was anticipated and which has its objective equivalent in the payment obligations made. The asset owner cannot, therefore, fully capitalize future tax payments in the sense of suffering all real burden at the moment of imposition under any conditions. There is nothing at all contradictory in this conclusion once the duality of cost in any choice is fully recognized. An anticipated cost is not and cannot be a substitute for a realized burden, nor can these two be dimensionally equivalent. "The coward dies a thousand deaths" before he dies.

5. Private and Social Cost

Equality between *marginal private cost* and *marginal social cost* is the allocative criterion of Pigovian welfare economics,[1] and the principle remains acceptable to most modern welfare economists. Corrective taxes and subsidies are deemed to be required in order to satisfy the necessary conditions for optimality when external effects are observed to be present. The subject of discussion here is limited to the cost conception that is implicit in the Pigovian policy criterion; for this reason, there is no need to review recent works in the theory of externality, as such, some of which place major qualifications on the Pigovian norms.[2] The purpose of this chapter is to demonstrate that the Pigovian principle embodies a failure to make the distinction between costs that may influence choice and costs that may be objectively measured.

Summary Analysis

Consider a standard example where the behavior of one person (or firm) exerts marginal external diseconomies on others than himself. These represent the loss of "goods" to others for which they are not compensated through ordinary market dealings. Application of the Pigovian norm suggests that the

---

1. The companion criterion, equality between marginal private product and marginal social product, reduces to the cost criterion when the latter is stated in opportunity-cost terms. The failure to take action that exerts external benefits can be treated as analytically equivalent to the taking of action that exerts external costs. In his own formulation, Pigou used the product terminology almost exclusively, although he referred to both types of divergence. See A. C. Pigou, *The Economics of Welfare* (4th ed.; London: Macmillan, 1932), esp. pp. 131–35.

2. Notably, R. H. Coase, "The Problem of Social Costs," *Journal of Law and Economics*, III (October 1960), 1–44; Otto A. Davis and Andrew Whinston, "Externality, Welfare, and the Theory of Games," *Journal of Political Economy*, LXX (June 1962), 241–62.

costs imposed externally on those who are not party to the decision-making should be brought within the calculus of the decision-maker. These costs should be added to the decision-maker's own internal costs, costs that he is presumed to take into account. The device often suggested is the levy of a tax on the performance of the externality-generating activity, a tax that is equated to the external costs per unit that the activity imposes. Other devices sometimes advanced are institutional arrangements designed to internalize the externality. In all cases, the purpose is to bring the costs that inform or influence the decision-maker into conformity with true "social" costs. The models remain individualistic in the sense that "social" costs are computed by a simple summation over individuals in the relevant community or group.

A Closer Look

According to the Pigovian theory, the change in "costs" which results from an explicitly recommended levy of a tax modifies the behavior of the acting person so that "efficiency" results. But what is meant by "costs" here? This Pigovian framework provides us with perhaps the best single example of confusion between classically derived objective cost concepts and the subjective cost concepts that influence individual choice.

Consider, first, the determination of the amount of the corrective tax that is to be imposed. This amount should equal the external costs that others than the decision-maker suffer as a consequence of decision. These costs are experienced by persons who may evaluate their own resultant utility losses: they may well speculate on what "might have been" in the absence of the external diseconomy that they suffer. In order to estimate the size of the corrective tax, however, some objective measurement must be placed on these external costs. But the analyst has no benchmark from which plausible estimates can be made. Since the persons who bear these "costs"—those who are externally affected—do not participate in the choice that generates the "costs," there is simply no means of determining, even indirectly, the value that they place on the utility loss that might be avoided. In the classic example, how much would the housewife whose laundry is fouled give to have the smoke removed from the air? Until and unless she is actually confronted with this choice, any estimate must remain almost wholly arbitrary. Smoke damage cannot be even remotely approximated by the estimated outlays that would be necessary to produce air "cleanliness." "Clean air" can, of course, be physically defined; the difficulty does not lie in the impossibility of defining units in a physically descriptive sense. Regardless of definition, however, "clean air" cannot be *exchanged* or *traded* among separate persons. Each person must simply adjust to the degree of air cleanliness that exists in his environment. There is no possibility of marginal adjustments over quantities of the "good" so as to produce an equilibrium that ensures against interpersonal differences in relative evaluations.

Figure 1 illustrates my argument. There is no way in which the analyst can objectively determine whether the housewife is at position A, B, or C on the diagram, yet it is clear that the utility loss, both at the margin and in total, may be significantly different in the three cases. There is no behavioral basis

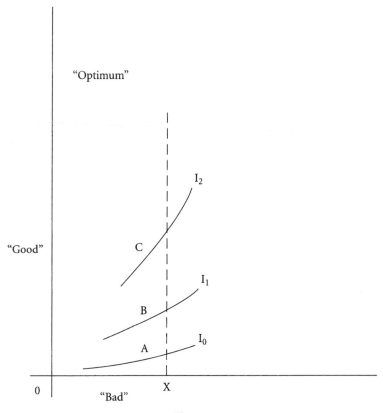

Figure 1

for observing evaluations here. Figure 1 also suggests that if individual preference functions have the standard properties, the valuations of separate persons probably vary directly with private-goods income. The affluent housewife will value clean air more highly than the poverty-stricken. The reason is obvious. The external diseconomy, "smoke damage," cannot be "retraded" among persons. If it could be, the poverty-stricken housewife might be quite willing to take on an extra share of the damage in exchange for some monetary payment from her affluent neighbor. But since such a trade cannot take place, she must simply adjust to the degree of "bads" in her environment.

Objective measurement of externally imposed costs seems more feasible in cases where the removal of the damaging agent results in changes in the production function of firms. If the damaged units should be producing firms, not individuals, there would seem to be no need to get into the complications of evaluating utility losses. A change in the rate of "pollution" can be observed to change the rate of outlay required for producing marketable goods and services. Since these goods and services command prices in markets, objective measurement of their value can be made.[3]

If a corrective tax, equal to the costs that are imposed externally upon others (which we shall now assume to be objectively measurable despite the problems noted above), is to generate the behavioral changes predicted by the Pigovian analysis, the internal costs as faced by the decision-maker must also be objectively measurable, at least indirectly. The analysis assumes implicitly that, in the absence of the corrective tax, choices are informed by money outlays made in purchasing inputs in ordinary market transactions. As an earlier discussion has shown, however, there is no logical support for this presump-

3. It seems likely that this helps to explain the source of the confusion. Marshall and Pigou developed the externality notion within the context of interfirm models, implicitly assuming competitive structures. As we shall see, the relevance of objectively measurable costs is limited even in this model, but the errors are of a different order of magnitude from those that arise when the externalities refer to an interpersonal interaction or to an interfirm interaction where utility functions are employed. The possibility of objectively measuring external costs does not, of course, ensure that the policy of levying a corrective tax is desirable. Under competition, this policy can be plausibly defended within certain limits. In noncompetitive structures, by contrast, the attempt to levy corrective taxes on an externality-generating firm may do more harm than good. On this elementary point, see my "External Diseconomies, Corrective Taxes, and Market Structure," *American Economic Review*, LIX (March 1969), 174–77.

tion in the general case. Observed money outlays need not reflect choice-influencing costs, the genuine opportunity costs that the decision-maker considers.

There is an obvious inconsistency. The Pigovian norm aims at bringing marginal private costs, *as these influence choice,* into line with social costs, *as these are objectively measured.* Only with objective measurability can the proper corrective devices be introduced. But under what conditions can objectively measurable costs, external and internal, be taken to reflect, with even reasonable accuracy, the costs that the effective decision-maker may take into account. In conditions of ideal competitive equilibrium, the costs that can be measured by the observer provide a reasonable proxy for the subjective evaluations of decision-makers. However, almost by definition, external effects are not imposed in such a setting.

Internal Costs, Equilibrium, and Quasi-Rents

The conditions under which these outlays may be taken to measure, even indirectly, the subjective barrier to choice must be carefully specified. These are as follows: (1) The individual, or firm, must be in full competitive equilibrium with respect to the activity that generates the external diseconomy; (2) at this equilibrium level of activity, and only at this level, losses are avoided and no profits are made; and (3) there are no profits in prospect of being made anywhere else in the economy. Under such conditions, the costs that may be *avoided* are simply the outlays that must be made. The individual, or firm, has available only one alternative loss-avoiding course of action which is that of not acting. In the latter, he avoids the outlay that the decision to act, considered in total or at the margin, requires. Not acting is clearly the most attractive alternative course of behavior here since all other alternatives must yield net losses.

It is important to note that quasi-rents cannot exist in the competitive equilibrium required in this model. The device of capitalizing differential resource capabilities into quasi-rents so as to equalize costs among separate firms cannot, therefore, be utilized. If it is to exist at all, the bridge between choice-influencing costs and objectively measurable outlays depends critically on the absence of quasi-rents. If such rents exist, either with respect to the personal behavior of an individual or with respect to the productive activity of a firm, there can be no presumption that anticipated outlay measures subjective opportunity costs, those that must influence actual choice behavior. The indirect linkage between subjective opportunity costs and objectively measured outlays which such equilibrium establishes is shattered. The reason is that in the presence of "quasi-rents," the individual or the firm has available more than one loss-avoiding alternative course of action. "Quasi-rents" or their equivalent provide a cushion which allows subjectively relevant elements of the decision calculus to become meaningful. As Frank Knight recognized, even if imperfectly, in his 1935 papers,[4] the allowance for any nonpecuniary aspects in the choice calculus of an individual or a firm plays havoc with the use of measurable outlays as surrogates for the opportunity costs that do, in fact, influence choice behavior. For our purposes at this point, the allowance of "quasi-rents" or their equivalent destroys the underlying logic of the Pigovian policy norms. There is simply no means to make an effective translation between the subjective opportunity costs that influence decision and the objectively measurable outlays that both the decision-taker and others who are externally affected undergo as a result of decision.

An Illustrative Example

Much of the critical analysis may be clarified by a simple illustrative example. Let us suppose that I enjoy foxhunting and that I maintain a kennel of hounds near my residence. I am considering adding one more hound to my already-large pack, and I know with reasonable accuracy the market price for hounds. This price is, let us say, $100.

My neighbor lives within sound range of my kennel, and he (and his family) will suffer some predictable utility loss if I decide to purchase the additional dog. For purposes of analysis here, let us say that this external damage can be reasonably evaluated at $45, presumably by an expert observer and also by both my neighbor and myself. Now let us suppose that I anticipate the incremental benefits of the additional dog at $160. This substantially exceeds the price of $100. Let us also assume that there are no alternative spend-

---

4. F. Knight, "Notes on Utility and Cost" (Mimeographed, University of Chicago, 1935). Published as two German articles in *Zeitschrift für Nationalökonomie* (Vienna), Band VI, Heft 1, 3 (1935).

ing outlets where I can secure net marginal benefits. In such circumstances, the opportunity costs arising from the enjoyments that I must avoid by the fact of making the outlay can roughly be measured at $100. However, in addition to these costs, I may well, in my calculus of decision, place some value on the enjoyments that my neighbor must also forego as a consequence of my purchasing the dog. His anticipated suffering, as well as my own, can be an obstacle to my decision.

Suppose that I try as best I can to place a value on this expected loss in utility for my neighbor and that I arrive at a figure of $45, which, as noted above, does roughly represent the value that he himself places on the action. The obstacle to my choice, my choice-influencing cost, will embody two elements. First, there is the evaluation of the alternative uses of the anticipated $100 outlay, which, under the conditions postulated, we measure at $100. Second, there is the evaluation that I place on the anticipated enjoyments that my neighbor must forego, in this case $45. Under such circumstances, I will proceed to carry out the purchase since the anticipated marginal benefits, $160, exceed the evaluation of foregone alternatives, $145.

Note that in the behavior postulated, I am acting in accordance with the Pigovian criterion, treated here as an *ethical norm for private behavior.* Quite literally, I am treating my neighbor as myself, and my internal decision calculus accurately reflects "marginal social cost" as the obstacle to decision, despite the absence of any corrective tax. Note also, however, that for the discrete choice in question, I shall be observed to impose an external cost on my neighbor for which I do not compensate him. If a Pigovian-trained economist should be called in to advise the government, he would likely recommend that I be subjected to a corrective tax, levied in the amount of the external costs, in this example $45. It is clear that, unless the components of my subjective opportunity costs are directly modified by such a tax, the effect will be to change my decision. Costs that a positive decision embody will now be approximated at $190. Facing these, I shall refrain from purchasing the hound despite the "social" or allocative distortion that my failure to do so generates. In this example, the corrective tax tends to convert a socially desirable choice outcome into a socially undesirable one.

My internal opportunity-cost components may be modified by the imposition of the tax. If I am fully aware that I am being taxed for the express reason that my behavior generates the external economy, I may reduce the valuation that I place on my neighbor's foregone enjoyment of silence. This reaction may be especially likely if the proceeds of the tax are earmarked for direct transfer to my neighbor. Such a direct linkage, and more importantly such a consciousness of the purpose of corrective taxes, has not been emphasized in the Pigovian literature and does not seem remotely descriptive of choice behavior. At best, we may acknowledge *some* substitution between the tax and the subjective valuation of the "external" component of opportunity cost; surely there is no reason to expect anything like a full offset.

In the simplified example, it is assumed that I value the foregone alternatives of others more or less equally with my own. This extreme altruism need not, of course, be assumed in order to reach the conclusion that the corrective tax produces inefficient outcomes. In the discrete choice discussed in the example, even if I place a valuation of *only $16* on the foregone enjoyment of my neighbor, the corrective tax of $45 will cause me to choose the inefficient outcome ($100 + $16 + $45 = $161 > $160). This valuation figure becomes even smaller as the personal "quasi-rent" or "marginal surplus" is reduced. Suppose, for example, that my estimate for marginal benefits is only $146, and that I place only a $2 valuation on the foregone enjoyment of my neighbor. My choice-influencing costs after the tax are then $147 ($100 + $2 + $45), which exceed my anticipated marginal benefits. I shall be led to the inefficient social choice, although the differential inefficiency here will be lower than in those cases where I place a somewhat higher valuation on the prospective utility losses of others.

Pigovian Economics and Christian Ethics

The example above suggests that a defense of the Pigovian policy norm's applicability may lie in the behavioral assumption that each person acts strictly in accordance with his own narrowly defined, materialistic "private" interest. His own behavior may be assumed to be wholly uninfluenced by the effects it exerts on other persons. Under such conditions, it might be argued, the demonstrated conflict between the corrective policy and the achievement of allocative efficiency would not arise. As the following section will show, even this restrictive assumption will not rescue the Pigovian analytics. At this point, however, the legitimacy of the assumption itself must be more carefully examined.

Initially, the behavioral assumption seems nothing more than an extension of the "economic man" who roams throughout predictive economic theory. Closer examination reveals, however, that the requirement here is much more restrictive than this. In the traditional neoclassical theory of markets, the implicit behavioral assumption is that of "nontuism," first clarified by Wicksteed. This is merely the assumption that, by and large and on the average, individuals or firms engaged in market-like behavior leave out of account the direct interests of those who are on the opposing side of the trading contract. The "economic man" of Wicksteed can adhere to a Christian ethic without neurosis, since he can, if he so chooses, incorporate in his behavior pattern some recognition of the interests of all his fellows except those with whom he is directly trading. He may continue to "love his neighbor," as long as his neighbor is not trading with him. In the externality relationship, by definition, trade does not take place. It seems reasonable to think that it is precisely in this kind of relationship that genuinely benevolent behavior patterns might be witnessed. Indeed, it might plausibly be argued that in almost all of our nonmarket behavior, there is potential externality and that the ordinary functioning of civil society depends critically on a certain mutuality of respect. When property rights are not well defined and, hence, market-like arrangements are difficult to establish, the very forms of behavior seem to pay at least lip service to something other than narrowly defined self-interest. "May I smoke?" provides a classic illustration.

The departures from behavior patterns based on narrowly materialistic utility functions seem to be almost universal only when *personal* externality relationships exist. That is to say, the argument against the narrow self-interest assumption applies fully only when the potential externality relationship is limited to a critically *small number of persons*. In large-number groups, by comparison, there may be little or no incorporation of the interests of "others" in the utility calculus of individuals. Here the individual really has no "neighbors," or may have none in any effective behavioral sense, despite the presence of "neighborhood effects." Under the latter conditions, the Pigovian logic and its policy implications are at least partially restored. The person who litters the nonresidential street in the large city probably does not worry much about the effects of his action on others. This suggests that, for such cases, the corrective devices implied by the Pigovian analysis should not generate conflicts with standard allocative norms provided, of course, that all of the other conditions required for their applicability are met.[5]

Narrow Self-Interest and Alternative-Opportunity Quasi-Rents

The preceding section indicated that one means of rescuing the Pigovian policy logic lies in making the explicit assumption that no factor involving "regard for others" influences the choices of the person who exerts external costs. Even with this constraint on individual utility functions, however, conflicts between applications of the policy norms and efficiency criteria will arise if prospective "quasi-rents" exist for alternative courses of action. This can also be shown in terms of the simple illustrative example already discussed.

In the earlier use of the example, we assumed that no "profit" prospects exist for any other spending opportunities. In this case and only in this case will the expected money outlay on resource inputs, $100, reflect at all accurately the internal component of genuine opportunity costs, and the expected

5. It is perhaps worth noting here the interesting difference in emphasis between political scientists and economists, both of whom discuss essentially the same behavioral interactions. In politics, primary emphasis has traditionally been placed on political obligation, on the duty of the individual to act in the "public interest." This represents an attempt to improve results through modifying the individual's utility function in the direction of causing him to place a higher valuation on the utilities of others. Relatively little attention has been given until quite recently to the prospects of making institutional changes that will channel private choice in the direction of producing more desirable social results.

In economics, by contrast, institutional or policy changes have been the center of attention, and relatively little discussion has been devoted to norms for individual behavior. As our analysis shows, economists have implicitly assumed that individuals act in accordance with quite narrowly defined self-interest, and they have developed policy norms which may prove inapplicable if this underlying behavioral postulate is not descriptive of reality.

For an earlier discussion of this difference between the two disciplines, see my "Marginal Notes on Reading Political Philosophy" included as Appendix I in James M. Buchanan and Gordon Tullock, *The Calculus of Consent* (Ann Arbor: University of Michigan Press, 1962; Paperback Edition, 1965).

marginal tax, $45, the comparable externally imposed component. In such a model, the added assumption that the choosing-acting person places no evaluation on either the utility levels attained by others or the changes in these levels that are the results of his own behavior will restore the consistency between the Pigovian policy logic and overall efficiency norms. What we now must show is that, even if we retain the narrowly defined self-interest assumption about individual behavior, any relaxation of the assumption about "profits" or "quasi-rents" in alternative courses of action will undermine the whole policy apparatus.

Consider the situation where there are anticipated "profit" prospects in alternative spending opportunities. Suppose that in considering the purchase of the additional foxhound, from which I estimate a marginal benefit of $160, I expect the outlay on resource inputs measured at $100, but that I also anticipate that I could invest $100 in some other line of activity yielding an expected marginal benefit which I subjectively value at $115. In this case, $115, and not $100, is the figure that best represents my choice-influencing opportunity cost, the barrier to choice, before the imposition of the tax. Suppose now that the corrective tax of $45 is levied on the marginal purchase, and, as before, let us accept that this accurately reflects my neighbor's own evaluation of the external damage that he will suffer from my action. It follows that "social costs"—those costs that must be borne by all members of the group and which are the result of the marginal choice—are best measured at $160. This figure reflects my own marginal opportunity costs, now measured at $115, plus the external costs borne by my neighbor, measured at $45. Because both the social costs and the social benefits of my acquiring another foxhound are measured at $160, the standard allocative norms suggest that I should be indifferent in the decision. Note, however, that this indifference will *not* be realized in my own choice calculus once the corrective tax is imposed on my marginal purchase. As I now confront the alternatives, my choice-influencing costs will be $166.75, not $160. Not only must I value the expected outlay on inputs in terms of the foregone alternatives, i.e., $115, but also, I must value the expected marginal tax outlay in terms of foregone alternatives which payment will make impossible to achieve. If the expected "profit" on the $100 outlay in an alternative course of action is $115, we should expect the choice-influencing costs of the expected $45 tax to be roughly $51.75. The choice is no longer marginal in my own decision calculus; the corrective tax has caused choice-influencing opportunity costs—*private* costs—to exceed marginal social costs. I shall overadjust my behavior, even considering the most restrictive self-interest arguments in my utility function.

Conclusion

I should emphasize that this chapter is not designed as a general critical analysis of the Pigovian policy norms. Such an analysis would have required the treatment of many interesting issues that have been ignored here. My purpose has been to utilize this familiar branch of applied economic theory to demonstrate the desirability of clarifying the basic notions of opportunity costs. To those who fully accept and understand the London-Austrian contributions, the internal inconsistencies in the Pigovian logic will be apparent. To those who have been trained in the neoclassical paradigms of opportunity cost, recognition of the inconsistencies may require a working out of elementary examples. It is not easy to question long-accepted precepts, and in the several versions of this chapter, I have found it difficult to prevent the analysis from lapsing into the kind of conventional methodology that I have often used in other works. The result may give the appearance of complexity despite the elementary nature of the points being made. In effect, the incorporation of the London conception of opportunity cost amounts to transforming one of the foundation stones of economic theory. Only when this basic modification is completed can real progress toward changing the superstructure be attempted on a large scale. Meanwhile, only the most exposed aspects of this superstructure—the Pigovian welfare analytics, for example—can be related directly to the particular flaw in one of the theory's cornerstones.

6. Cost Without Markets

If prices are established in a market process, the decisions of buyers and sellers will be based on cost-benefit comparisons. Before any choice is made, anticipated benefits must exceed opportunity cost. If continuous adjustment is possible, each participant moves toward behavioral equilibrium where anticipated marginal benefit equals marginal opportunity cost. In this purely individualistic context, questions about the precise meaning of cost or of benefit need not arise. The analysis offers a logic of rational individual decision, and cost is simply that which is foregone by positive choice, at the moment of choice itself.

As Hayek emphasized, equilibrium in a market interaction is categorically different from the behavioral equilibrium of an individual participant in that interaction. In the latter, there must be an absence of gains-from-trade *within* the perceived choice range of the individual. In the former, there must be an absence of gains-from-trade, in total or at the margin, from action taken *among* all individuals, each one of whom perceives the prospects of trade with others as a part of his own choice set. In order for market equilibrium to be established, every participant must be in his own behavioral equilibrium, but the contrary need not be true. That is, each individual can attain behavioral equilibrium at the moment of choice, but unless the decisions of separate persons are in a unique relationship with one another, market equilibrium need not *result*. The failure of this equilibrium to emerge will set in motion changes in behavioral equilibria of individuals for subsequent choices.

Prices, Costs, and Market Equilibrium

What are the relationships between "prices" and "costs" in full market equilibrium? For each participant, expected marginal benefit will be equal to marginal opportunity cost, both measured in terms of the individual's subjective valuation. All persons are observed to confront uniform relative prices for goods; this is a necessary condition for the elimination of gains-from-trade. Since each participant is in full behavioral equilibrium, it follows that each person must confront the same marginal cost. As a demander, the individual adjusts his purchases to ensure that anticipated marginal benefit equals price. Hence, the anticipated marginal benefits of a good, measured in the numeraire, are equal for all demanders. As a supplier, the individual adjusts his sales to ensure that anticipated opportunities foregone, marginal opportunity cost, equals price. Hence, marginal opportunity cost, measured in the numeraire, is equal for all suppliers.

Prices tend to equal marginal opportunity costs in full market equilibrium. But costs here are fully analogous to marginal benefits on the demand side. *Only prices have objective, empirical content;* neither the marginal evaluations of the demanders nor the marginal costs of the suppliers (the marginal evaluations of foregone alternatives) can be employed as a basis for determining prices. The reason is that these are both brought into equality with prices by behavioral adjustments on both sides of the market. Prices are not brought into equality with some objectively determinable and empirically measurable phenomena, on either the demand or the supply side of the market.

In this elementary logic of the market process, we are back in the classical model for goods with fixed supply, the model that became the general one with the advent of the subjective-value theory. There is no "theory" of normal exchange value with positive content here. The analysis provides an "explanation" of results, a logic of interaction; it contains no predictive hypotheses.

Resource-Service Prices as Final-Product Costs

Final goods are not available in fixed quantities, however, and with the introduction of resource services, the objectivity of cost tends to be reintroduced. Prices for productive services are established in a market process, and these, like the prices for final goods, are empirically observable. These resource-service prices are derived from the evaluations placed on final products, which are acknowledged to be based on subjective elements. But the whole market acts to establish observable prices, and these prices, in turn, seem to make the *costs* of final products objectively real. The costs of production as faced by producing firms are also the prices of resource units as received by supplying agents. For final-product markets, therefore, supply-side adjustments seem to offer an escape from the logic into empirical reality. Suppliers act so as to bring costs into equality with prices; costs represent the marginal evaluations of foregone alternatives as expressed by the whole market and as expressed in money terms. For the prices of final products at least, we seem to be back in the quasi-classical world of one-way causality.

Even in full market equilibrium, however, the objectivity of opportunity cost is only apparent. As Frank Knight correctly indicated in his 1934 and 1935 papers, even in full equilibrium, resource-service prices reflect costs only if nonpecuniary advantages or disadvantages are absent from the choices of resource-supplying agents. If pecuniary returns provide the sole motivation for resource suppliers, the observed price for a resource unit does represent the choice-influencing opportunity cost of that unit, even if indirectly. If, on the other hand, nonpecuniary elements are present in the decisions of resource suppliers, the choice-influencing cost of the resource units is not observable in money prices paid for resources. The apparent linkage between final-product cost, in some objective sense, and observed prices paid for resource services disappears.

This does not, of course, affect the standard analysis of market interaction, and it does nothing to modify the welfare inferences that may be drawn from an understanding of competitive adjustment. So long as individuals on either side of the market are allowed to express their preferences by continuous adjustments in behavior, nonpecuniary elements will be fully embodied in the solution that emerges. Prices will tend to equal marginal opportunity costs. What is destroyed by the presence of nonpecuniary elements in choice is the spurious objectivity of costs, as measured by prices of resource services.

These prices may embody nonpecuniary elements, however, for only some resource suppliers, and not necessarily for all. If there exist a sufficient number of suppliers who are on the margin of indifference among all employments yielding equivalent pecuniary returns, resource-service prices accurately represent *marginal* opportunity costs despite inframarginal suppliers who are known to choose on the basis of nonpecuniary as well as pecuniary rewards. Inframarginally, nonpecuniary elements in choice do not affect the relationship between observed resource-service prices and marginal costs of final products. This applies only to marginal costs, however; average costs will not be accurately measured by observed outlays on resource inputs. Even if nonpecuniary elements are not present in effective choices made at the margin of adjustment and, hence, are not included in marginal opportunity costs, the presence of nonpecuniary elements in choices made over infra-marginal ranges of supply ensures that observed outlays will not measure to-tal costs. This does not modify the allocative results of the market interaction process, but it does mean that the use of predicted or observed outlays to measure total costs—costs which are to be compared with expected benefits as a basis for making nonmarket allocative decisions—can lead to serious error.

Market Equilibrium, Costs, and Quasi-Rents

In the absence of nonpecuniary elements in resource suppliers' choices, ob-served outlays on resource services would seem to provide an objective, even if indirect, measurement of the choice-influencing opportunity costs to these suppliers if the system is in full competitive equilibrium. The conditions for equilibrium that are required in this context are, however, much more severe than those that are necessary for other purposes. *All* resource suppliers must be on a margin of indifference among alternative employments; quasi-rents cannot be present. If some resource units earn quasi-rents, observed outlays on resource services will not accurately reflect the choice-influencing costs of resource owners with regard to the interoccupational or interindustry choices.

Resource-service prices are set at the appropriate margins of employment, and competition among purchasers causes similar units to earn similar re-turns. Similarity in internal or intraindustry productivity does not, however, imply similarity in alternative employment or interindustry productivity. Re-sources may be differentially specialized to particular industries. When this happens, quasi-rents emerge. The existence of such quasi-rents does not, of course, violate the logic of market interaction. In equilibrium, prices will be equal to costs, but costs must be tied to the particular decisions that are made. In selling his services to a *single* firm within a competitive industry, the resource owner foregoes a return that he might secure from any other firm in the same industry. Quasi-rents are not present in this situation since the resource owner is indifferent among employment by different firms. However, the choice of employment within the industry generally, as against other industries, may take place in the presence of quasi-rents. The foregone earnings outside the industry may fall short of those that may be secured from any single firm within the industry. Prices will, therefore, be equal to the costs that inform *within-industry* choices. For all except the marginal supplier, however, the prices paid for resource services—the outlays—will exceed the marginal evaluation of prospective alternative returns foregone outside the industry, even in full market equilibrium.

The existence of such inframarginal quasi-rents does not modify allocative outcomes of the market process because these quasi-rents disappear at the margin. For both an interfirm and an interindustry decision, the marginal resource supplier is in full equilibrium. Observed outlay made to him by the firm accurately measures his evaluation of foregone alternatives. The receipt of quasi-rents by inframarginal suppliers was the subject of a major debate a half-century ago, and one of the contributions of Allyn Young was that of showing the irrelevance of these for allocative efficiency.

Problems do emerge, however, when any attempt is made to utilize the properties of the market process as guidelines or norms for the making of nonmarket decisions. In this extension, the relationship between inframarginal quasi-rents and "costs" must be kept in mind.

The Cost of Military Manpower: An Example

An example may illustrate some of the points put forth in this chapter. Let us suppose that the government calls upon an economist for expert advice. It asks him to estimate the "cost" of securing military manpower of specified quality and in specified quantity. The comparison of benefit estimates with this "cost" presumably will form the basis for making allocative decisions concerning the amount of military manpower to be employed. To simplify the problem, assume that a fixed number of common soldiers is needed. These are units that are homogeneous for the military purposes for which they are required.

In Figure 2, let us depict the actual supply curve for common soldiers as S, and let us say that X is the quantity needed. The supply curve, which we shall assume is accurately known to the consultant, represents a schedule of

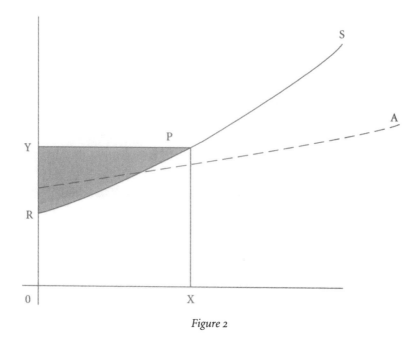

Figure 2

minimum prices (wages) that would be required to bring forth the several quantities indicated. Initially, let us also presume that all prospective soldiers are motivated solely by the prospect of pecuniary rewards. In this case, the curve S also represents the returns that these prospective military men forego in alternative lines of employment. The fact that the supply curve slopes upward indicates differential productivity in alternative employments despite the homogeneity of units in producing military services.

If the government is presumed to act as if it were a fully competitive industry in purchasing military manpower, its prospective outlay is measured by the rectangle 0XPY. This outlay overstates the "costs" that are involved in the prospective occupational choices, however, because of the inframarginal quasi-rents. The shaded area, RPY, is not a part of total costs in any choice-influencing sense. If the amount represented by this area is included in the cost side of a cost-benefit comparison, the result will be biased against resource commitment in this usage. Providing only that the government relies on contractual purchase agreements, this conclusion holds regardless of the means through which the government purchases its military force. If, for equity reasons, the government pays a uniform wage to all soldiers, despite the emergence of inframarginal quasi-rents, outlay will be greater than "costs," but a part of outlay will now represent a by-product of the resource commitment. Unless this is recognized in the cost-benefit computation, too few resources will be allocated to all increasing supply-price public facilities or projects. The use of predicted outlay to measure "costs" in this situation would reflect the Pigovian error that Young effectively exposed.

If nonpecuniary elements are present in the occupational choices of resource suppliers, the supply curve no longer measures the earnings of prospective soldiers in other employments. Some such curve may be derived, say A in Figure 2, which does reflect alternative pecuniary earnings. As drawn, the curve of alternative returns in relation to the "true" supply curve suggests that nonpecuniary differentials shift from positive to negative over increasing quantity. This presents a more serious difficulty to the economist who must estimate costs than that which the presence of inframarginal quasi-rents presents. When nonpecuniary aspects of choice can be assumed away, the area under the actual supply curve does reflect "costs," and this area can be roughly approximated from observed data on earnings in alternative employments. With nonpecuniary elements in the picture, however, no such indirect means of approximating choice-influencing costs exists. Whether or not some estimate of alternative earnings will over- or understate costs will depend on the quantity that is specified. As drawn in Figure 2, an overestimate would result for quantities toward the left of the quantity range, and an underestimate for quantities toward the right.

All of the measures of costs so far discussed, direct or indirect, assume meaning only if the government *purchases* the resource units in a series of contractual market-like arrangements with the individuals who are to supply the services. The soldiers must voluntarily sell their services. If the actual recruitment of soldiers takes place in any other manner, the cost considerations discussed here must be re-examined. In the absence of nonpecuniary elements in choice for every one of the men conscripted, the opportunity costs of a conscripted military force would be measured by the earnings that members of this force could secure in nonmilitary employments.[1] This would

---

1. This definition of the opportunity costs of conscription is advanced by George Stigler in his highly respected textbook in microeconomic theory. Stigler says, "The cost of a

imply that each member of the force would be indifferent between military and nonmilitary employment if earnings in military employment were equivalent to those in nonmilitary pursuits. As noted earlier, this is a much more restrictive requirement than that which is needed to eliminate the significance of nonpecuniary elements for allocative decisions within a market-like process. In the latter, nonpecuniary elements need not modify the allocative results so long as a sufficient number of marginal adjusters remain indifferent to the nonpecuniary differences among the separate employments. If foregone earnings are to measure choice-influencing costs, however, this indifference must be manifested for every resource supplier, not just for those who are the marginal adjusters. The disappearance of nonpecuniary elements in choice at the freely adjusted margins of behavior, like the disappearance of quasi-rents at the margins, restores the allocative relevance of resource-service prices as proximate measures for *marginal opportunity costs*. But this is helpful only if resource services are purchased through ordinary contractual arrangements.

The Cost of Crime: Another Example

Economists have only recently started to pay attention to crime and punishment, but this now bids fair to becoming a relatively important research area. Several studies have involved the extension of economic analysis to the decisions of criminals on the one hand and to those of law enforcement agencies on the other, both of which kinds of decisions are clearly outside a market equilibrium context. The implication of my discussion is that any costs which the economist may objectify need bear little relation to those costs which serve as actual obstacles to decisions. Recognition of this fact need not destroy the usefulness of the economic analysis. The costs that the economist quantifies may be directionally related to those costs that inhibit choice. In this case, changes in the level of objectified costs (for example, changes in the probabilities of conviction and in the severity of punishment) will produce effects on the number of offenses committed. Serious problems arise here

---

soldier for an economy, however, is his foregone product as a civilian, and this is not directly affected by his rate of pay." See George Stigler, *The Theory of Price* (3rd ed.; New York: Macmillan, 1966), p. 106.

only when the attempt is made to lay down more explicit norms for policy, as, for example, when the conditions for optimality or efficiency are discussed.

One part of Gary Becker's recent, and excellent, paper may be used as an example.[2] In a section in which he discusses optimality conditions, Becker argues that if the costs of apprehending and convicting offenders are zero, the marginal value of the fines imposed on criminals should be equated to the marginal value of the harm that offenses cause. This is an admittedly limited model, but, even here, Becker's conclusion is valid only under a special assumption about the prospective criminal's choice behavior. In contemplating an offense, the criminal must be assumed to leave out of account any and all considerations of the harm imposed on others. It must be assumed that this does not enter as an obstacle in his decision, that this is not a part of his choice-influencing cost. If, for any reason, this element enters as a genuine cost, Becker's suggested norm would overshoot the mark. Some crimes that would be in the "social interest" would be prevented by the imposition of Becker's conditions. (The analysis here is almost identical to that made in an earlier chapter with reference to the Pigovian analysis.) Perhaps more significantly, the optimal number of offenses would be secured when marginal fines remain considerably lower than the marginal damage to others. In other words, for the criminal who incorporates into his costs some consideration of the harm his crime will impose on others, the point at which "crime may not pay" him is reached well before the point at which the observing economist marks the disappearance of net profit.

Clarification of the cost concept may have certain interesting and relatively important policy implications for criminal activity, or even for noncriminal activity that is for any reason held to be suspect or immoral. To the extent that the consideration of prospective harm to others, or, in fact, any moral restraint upon the decision, varies with the location and incidence of the offense contemplated, the opportunity cost of the offense varies. Hence, we should expect that crimes committed within the local community of the perpetrator against persons with whom he has close contacts would normally involve a higher cost barrier due to the moral restraint upon the actor

2. Gary Becker, "Crime and Punishment: An Economic Approach," *Journal of Political Economy*, 76 (March–April 1968), 169–217.

in such a situation. From this it follows that fines or penalties required to achieve any given level of deterrence can be somewhat lower for these cases than for others. That is, crimes committed locally should bear lower fines than those imposed for identical crimes committed outside the community and on "foreigners." Other similar implications can be derived. Generally, punishments and fines for comparable crimes can be lower in small cities than in large. And, importantly, punishments for crimes against persons or property of the same racial or religious group can be lower than punishments for identical crimes against persons who are members of ethnic or religious groups differing from those to which the criminal belongs.

Artificial Choice-Making

The most serious problem in extending the basic allocative meaning of choice-influencing opportunity cost to decisions that must be made outside the market process has been ignored to this point. The preceding discussion was limited to an examination of the meaning of cost in a nonmarket context and to some difficulties in estimation. The problem of choice-making itself was not raised here, although it was treated briefly in Chapter 4.

In the military manpower illustration presented earlier, we presumed, without critical scrutiny, that if costs could somehow be estimated, the choices that were finally to be made would be based upon these. This tends to remove all behavioral content from choosing behavior, however, and it is essential that the distinction between "true costs" and "costs that influence nonmarket choice" be clarified. The basic point to be emphasized is a simple one: costs that are relevant for the making of decisions must be those that relate to the decisions made. The very nature of nonmarket choice ensures that "costs" cannot be those that are confronted in market choice.

The employment of resource services in any manner involves a cost to the resource owners; this cost consists in their own evaluation of foregone alternatives, an evaluation made at the moment of commitment. This is the "true" opportunity cost that comes to be embodied in the market process, and it is this cost, at least at the margins of adjustment, which is brought into line with prices of final products. Allocative efficiency is the result. In this interaction, however, all choices are made by demanders and suppliers, each of whom is responsible for the results of his behavior. The resource owner who decides to commit his services to occupation A rather than to occupation B lives with this decision. To the extent that his own utility influences his behavior, he is under pressure to make "correct" decisions, since his utility will be the magnitude affected by the making of "incorrect" decisions. If a market decision-maker fails to take advantage of prospective opportunities, opportunities which later are revealed as highly desirable, he suffers the sensation of opportunity losses. Those experiences that "might have been" will be recognized as his own losses.

This decision structure cannot be present with nonmarket choice. If the "true costs" of employing resources could be measured (let us say by an omniscient observer who can read all preference functions) along with the "true benefits," allocative efficiency in nonmarket resource usage could be ensured only if the effective decision-maker acted in accordance with *artificial* criteria for choice. That is to say, allocative efficiency will emerge only if the effective choice-maker acts, not as a behaving person, but as a rule-following automaton. The distinction here has been widely recognized, and it is as old as the Aristotelian defense of private property. It has not, however, effectively and critically informed the core of economic analysis, largely, I submit, because of the confusion in elementary cost theory. Only recently in the efforts of those scholars (such as Alchian, Coase, Demsetz, McKean, and Tullock) who have begun to develop the rudiments of an economic theory of property do we find explicit examination of the relationship between the predicted outcomes and the decision structure within which the choices are made.

Socialist Calculation and Socialist Choice

The Austrians and pseudo-Austrians—Mises, Hayek, and Robbins—who were involved in disputing the possibility of socialist calculation in the great interwar debate were all contributors to the evolution of opportunity-cost theory and implicitly acknowledged the basic distinction emphasized here. This particular aspect of their argument tended to be obscured, however, by their relative overemphasis on the difficulties in *calculation* that prospective socialist decision-makers would face. These difficulties are, of course, extremely important, and the information problems that centralized economic planning confronts are indeed enormous, as experience has surely proved. Relatively speaking, however, the more significant criticism of socialist economic organization lies in the difficulties of choice-making. Even if the socialist state should somehow discover an oracle that would allow all calculations to be made perfectly, even if all preference functions are revealed, and even if all production functions are known with certainty, efficiency in allocation will emerge only if the effective decision-makers are converted into economic eunuchs. Only if such men can be motivated to behave, to make decisions in accordance with cost criteria that are different from *their own,* can this decision-structure become workable. This amounts to saying that even if the problems of calculation are totally disregarded, the socialist system will generate efficiency in results only if men can be trained to make choices that do not embody the opportunity costs that they, individually and personally, confront.

The contrast between the implicit behavioral assumptions made by those who have proposed the Pigovian corrective taxes and subsidies in the face of external diseconomies and economies and the implicit behavioral assumptions made by those who argued that socialist organization can produce efficient results is striking. As noted in Chapter 5, for the Pigovian policy proposals to accomplish their own stated purposes, individuals who generate externalities must behave so as to maximize their own narrowly conceived economic interests. The effects of their own behavior on the predicted utility levels of others than themselves cannot be assumed to influence their behavior. By comparison, the idealized manager of the socialist enterprise must be assumed to act solely on the basis of nonindividualistic criteria. His own utility cannot be allowed to influence the decisions that he makes; he must choose in accordance with the costs and benefits predicted for the whole community; and his own position in the community must be treated as if it were the same as that of any other member. Whereas the Pigovian man must be strictly *Homo economicus* in the narrowest sense, the socialist bureaucrat must be *non–Homo economicus* in the purest sense. Both men can be only caricatures of actual persons, but both have been present in much serious discussion of real-world policy.

The contrast in the behavioral assumptions implicit in these two related bodies of literature is striking in itself, but even more interesting for our purposes is the common source of the confusion. In their contrasting ways, both the Pigovian policy correctives and the idealized socialist economy are intellectual products of cost-theory confusion. Both find their roots in classical economics, with its objectification of costs. Only if costs can be objectified can they be divorced from choice, and only if they are divorced from choice can the institutional-organizational setting that the chooser inhabits have no influence on costs. In the socialist scheme of things, costs are derived from physical relations among inputs and outputs. These may be externally measured, and these measurements can provide the basis for the rules that are laid down for managers of enterprises. Valuation enters the calculus only as the consuming public, through their behavior, establish demand prices, which become objective realities once established. The subjective valuation that must inform every choice is neglected.

Costs in Bureaucratic Choice

Bureaucratic decision-makers are human beings. This simple fact is only now beginning to be acknowledged in the theories of bureaucracy.[3] The individual who is confronted with a choice among alternatives must choose, and the cost that inhibits decision is his own evaluation of the alternative that must be foregone. Rules can be laid down which direct him to adopt criteria that reflect the underlying economic realities. In a world of complete certainty, there is no decision problem. A computer can make all "choices," if indeed "choices" exist. One of the central confusions leading to the false objectification of costs has been the extension of the perfect knowledge assumption of competitive equilibrium theory to the analysis of nonequilibrium choices, whether made in a market or a nonmarket process. Genuine choice is confronted only in a world of uncertainty, and, of course, all economic choices are made in this context. Any analysis of bureaucratic choice must be based on a recognition of this simple fact.

It will be helpful to construct the simplest possible model. Assume that a civil servant must decide between only two courses of action, *a* and *b*. These may be anything, including the production of n or $n + 1$ units of output. Either of two possible external events may accompany this action, event x or y. Again these may take almost any form, including the state of consumer demand at the margin. Further, let us assume that the total payoff to the

3. See Gordon Tullock, *The Politics of Bureaucracy* (Washington, D.C.: Public Affairs Press, 1965).

	x	y
a	100	20
	(6)	(2)
b	50	60
	(4)	(5)

Figure 3

community under each of the four possible outcomes is accurately estimated and that these are indicated by the large numbers in the four cells of Figure 3.[4]

The choice between a and b will depend, of course, on the subjective probabilities assigned to x and y. Let us assume that the choosing agent assigns each event an equal probability. From the arithmetic, it is then clear that the expected value to the whole community will be higher from a than from b. However, with a change in the probability coefficients, from (.5, .5) to (.4, .6), the expected value to the community becomes higher from b than from a. In genuine uncertainty, the decision-maker must assign such subjective probabilities; there is no objectively determinable set of coefficients. When this is recognized, it is clear that there is simply no means of evaluating the choosing agent's performance externally and after choice. Each of two separate persons may choose differently when confronted with identical sets of alternatives. There is no "correct" choice independent of the subjective probabilities that are assigned. In our example, one chooser may reject b because its cost exceeds expected returns; the other may reject a for the same reason. There is no way that an external observer or auditor can, *ex post*, decide which of the two persons followed "the rules" more closely.

This difficulty in evaluating the efficiency of nonmarket decision-making suggests that the institutional pattern of rewards and punishments may be modified to ensure that, regardless of the choices that are made, the chooser will have some personal incentive to perform in accordance with "social" maximization criteria. This will substitute *ex ante* motivation for individual

---

4. These estimates are necessarily *ex ante:* only one outcome can be actually observed after choice.

behavior in the "public interest" for the misguided and hopeless efforts at judging or auditing the results *ex post*. The necessity for some coordination between the cost-benefit structure as confronted by the decision-maker and the "true" cost-benefit structure of the whole community has, by this time, come to be widely recognized both in theory and in practice.

This institutional device is necessarily limited, however, and for several reasons it cannot fully resolve the dilemma of nonmarket economic choice. Nonmarket choice cannot, by its very nature, be made to duplicate market choice until and unless the ownership-responsibility pattern in the former fully matches that in the latter, an achievement that would, of course, eliminate all institutional differences between the two.

Suppose, as an initial example, that an individual cost-benefit structure is introduced as shown by the single-bracketed terms in Figure 3. Ordinally, at least, the relative payoffs to the decision-maker coincide with those for the community. However, if he assigns equal subjective probabilities to x and to y, his own cost-benefit calculation will lead him to select b, not a. The numerical array is, of course, deliberately designed to indicate this result, but it should be evident that ordinal equivalence between the payoff structure of the decision-maker and that of the whole community is not sufficient to ensure consistency in choices.

Proportionality is suggested. If the personal payoffs to the decision-maker, negative or positive, are made strictly proportional to those of the whole community, then choices made in accordance with expected-value criteria will produce the required coordination. At this point, the relevance of expected-value maximization as a rule for individual choice behavior must be called into question. It is well established that an individual will maximize present value only if he derives no utility or disutility from risk-taking and if the marginal utility of income to him is constant over the relevant outcome range. If the marginal utility of income declines over this range and if the chooser is neither a risk averter nor a risk preferrer, he will tend to have some preference for the safer of the two alternatives, some "nonpecuniary" differential in favor of alternative b in the numerical illustration of Figure 3. The question that then emerges is whether or not this nonpecuniary differential faced by the decision-maker whose payoffs are proportional to those for the whole community need be the same as that which "should" inform the decision made from the community's point of view. As Domar and Musgrave pointed out in another connection,[5] the individual whose payoff structure is only some proportionate share of that which he might confront under full ownership will tend to take *more* risks. The reason is obvious. Since the nonpecuniary differential arises only because of the declining marginal utility of income, the fact that the outcome range is lower under proportionate share payoffs than under full responsibility and ownership ensures some lessening of this differential.

An additional and important element tends to work in the opposing direction. Given a structure of individual payoffs that are only proportional to total community payoffs, the absolute differences between the expected value of alternatives are lower for the decision-maker than for the community; and the differences in the opportunity costs of two separate alternatives are lower. Considering this, it seems evident that behavior will tend to be less responsive to changes in the underlying conditions under bureaucratic choice than under market choice. The decision-maker in the latter situation cannot perceive changes in signals with the same sensitivity as he could in the former for the simple reason that the signals are stronger in the first case. If we also recognize and allow for threshold-sensitive response in behavior generally, this differential in behavior becomes even more pronounced.[6]

These separate elements emphasize the fact that proportionality between the decision-maker's cost-benefit matrix and that of the community will not ensure an approximation to market-choice results in a regime of bureaucratic choice. Costs as confronted by the choosing agents must remain inherently different in the two decision structures, and it is these differences that constitute the basic problem of securing efficiency in nonmarket choice-making.

5. E. D. Domar and R. A. Musgrave, "Proportional Income Taxation and Risk-Taking," *Quarterly Journal of Economics*, LVIII (May 1944), 388–422, reprinted in American Economic Association, *Readings in the Economics of Taxation* (Homewood, Ill.: Richard D. Irwin, 1959), pp. 493–524.

6. Devletoglou has argued persuasively that all human behavior must be analyzed in terms of a threshold-sensitive model. See Nicos Devletoglou and P. A. Demetriou, "Choice and Threshold: A Further Experiment in Spatial Duopoly," *Economica*, XXXIV (November 1967), 351–71.

Author Index

Subject Index

abstinence, 7, 8
Austrian economics, xi, 20, 23, 87

benefit-cost analysis, 54, 56
burden: and cost, 50

capitalization: of taxes, 63–64
choice: and cost, 17, 19, 20, 37–48; in
   economics, 40; logic, 40; and
   opportunity cost, 16. *See also* cost
Christian ethics, 72–74
comparative advantage, 8
cost-benefit analysis, 54, 56
cost(s): and burden, 40; in bureaucratic
   choice, 89–90; in business decisions,
   26–29; and choice, 20, 23, 37–48, 41,
   42–44; in classical economics, 3; of
   crime, 84–86; of debt-financed outlay,
   59–63; dimensions, 41; as displaced
   value, 20; in economic theory, 3–16;
   and entrepreneurship, 18; as ephemeral,
   30; and equilibrium, 46–48; as forward-
   looking, 41; incidence, 46; location, 41;
   London tradition, 17–36; in market
   equilibrium, 77–78; meanings, xiv,
   42–46; measurability, 41; and
   nonmarket value, 15; objective, 24; and
   pain, 8, 44; and political structure,
   53–55; and pricing rules, 31; private, 65;
   of production, theory, 5–6, 17; and
   profit maximization, 27–28; and public
   debt, 59–63; in public finance theory,

xiv; of public goods, 49–64; and quasi-
   rents, 80–81; real, 7; realization, 41; and
   sacrifice, 8, 43–44; social, 32, 65–76; in
   socialist calculation, 87–89; sunk,
   45–46; in tax incidence, 50–52; in
   welfare economics, 25
crime: cost of, 84–86

debt: and cost, 59–63
dictatorship: and cost, 55
dimensionality of cost, 41

economic man, 38
economics: as logic of choice, 40; as
   predictive science, 37–40
entrepreneurship and cost, 18
equilibrium: and cost, 77–78
ethics: in Pigovian economics, 71–74
excess burden, 50

falsification, 5, 10, 37–40

Homo economicus, 38, 49, 88

incidence: of debt-financed outlay, 59–63;
   of taxes, 50–52

London cost tradition, 17–36
London School of Economics (LSE),
   17–36

Malthusian theory of population, 7
marginal-cost pricing, 29 n

This book is set in Minion, a typeface designed by Robert Slimbach specifically for digital typesetting. Released by Adobe in 1989, it is a versatile neohumanist face that shows the influence of Slimbach's own calligraphy.

This book is printed on paper that is acid-free and meets the requirements of the American National Standard for Permanence of Paper for Printed Library Materials, z39.48-1992. ⊗

Book design by Louise OFarrell, Gainesville, Fla.
Typography by Impressions Book and Journal Services, Inc., Madison, Wisc.
Printed and bound by Sheridan Books, Chelsea, Mich.